Unless otherwise noted, all scriptural citations are from the New King James Translations 1990, 1985, 1983, Thomas Nelson, Nashville, Tn.

978-1-937501-10-5   1-937501-10-8

Produced by JaDon Management Inc.
1405 4th Ave. N. W. #109
Ardmore, Ok. 73401

Original Cover Art by
Jeff McCormack

# Acknowledgements

My sincere appreciation to Sam Dawson, a fine author in his own right, for generating my topical and scripture indices. I have not yet mastered that fine art, so I appreciate so much his efforts to make this book more "user friendly."

Likewise, my thanks to Jack Gibbert, a sharp eyed proof reader, who has truly made this book far more correct grammatically. Any remaining errata are my fault.

My thanks to many others unnamed who have offered suggestions and comments that resulted in the inclusion of certain materials and thoughts. Included is the suggestion to incorporate footnotes instead of end notes. I have done this on a few books now and the positive feedback is appreciated.

My thanks in advance to all those who have Berean hearts and minds willing to listen and think. Traditionalism is very, very strong. Creedalism and church history lamentably mean more to some people than scripture itself. To those brave souls willing to think for themselves and whose only concern is *Sola Scriptura*, my sincere thanks is offered.

As always, my deepest thanks to my wonderful wife for her patience as I work on projects like this "twenty four seven." I tend to be very focused, not easily distracted from the project of the moment, which results in my being, a "selective hearer" at times. She is always wonderfully understanding, and supportive of my work.

Don K. Preston (D. Div.)
President Preterist Research Institute
www.eschatology.org
www.bibleprophecy.com
www.donkpreston.com
2013

# Table of Contents
## Fifteen Reasons Why AD 70 Was Not A Type of the "Real" End

Reason #1 - Pages 15-20
The Old Testament prophets never foretold two ends of two ages, two kingdoms, two resurrections or two last days.

Reason #2 - Pages 21-29
The Christian age has no end. Thus, the end of the Old Covenant age could not be typological of the end of what is endless!

Reason #3 - Pages 30-35
Types Are Always *Inferior*– Anticipating Something *Better*– and There Is Nothing Better than the Work of Christ in the Church

Reason #4 - Pages 36-42
No New Testament writer ever said the events of their day were typological of greater events to come.

Reason #5 - Pages 43-48
Jesus said the events of AD 70 were the greatest that had ever been, or that ever would be (Matthew 24:21). So, how can the greatest events in history, foreshadow events that are even greater?

Reason #6 - Pages 49-58
Jesus Said the Events of AD 70 Would Be When "All Things That Are Written must Be Fulfilled" (Luke 21:22). This Means There Could Not Be Any Additional Eschatology Beyond Ad 70.

Reason #7– Pages 59-67
The Restoration of All Things Would Be Consummated at the Parousia– Which Would Be At the End of the Old Covenant Age of Israel

Reason #8 - Pages 68-78
Paul Said the Goal of All the Previous Ages Had Come in His Generation (1 Corinthians 10:11).

Reason #9 - Pages 79-95
Then Comes The End – The End of 1 Corinthians 15 Cannot Be the End of Christ's rule or the end of Time.

Reason #10 - Pages 96-104
Ephesians 1:10 - "That in the stewardship of the fulness of time He would gather together all things in one body, in Christ."

Reason #11 - Pages 105-114
Entrance into the Most Holy Place– Restoration to the Edenic Presence - The Eschatological Goal Was to Be at the End of the Old Covenant Age– Not the End of the Christian Age (Hebrews 9:6-10).

Reason #12 - Pages 115-131
The First Century Church Had Arrived at Zion– The Locus of the Eschatological, End of the Millennium Resurrection.

Reason #13 - Pages 132-140
The Judgment of the Living and the Dead Occurred in AD 70 - The Kingdoms of the World Became the Kingdom of God and His Christ.

Reason #14 - Pages 141-152
The Millennium Ended in AD 70.

Reason #15 - Pages 153-179
If the Events of AD 70 Were Typological of a Future End of the Age, Then Christ Will Divorce and Destroy the Church, as an Unfaithful Bride That Has Become a Harlot and Will Marry Another Bride– Under (Another) New Covenant.

Summary and Conclusion - 180-186

Indices - 188ff

# AD 70: A Shadow
# of the (Real) End?

## Was the End of the Age in
## AD 70  A Type or Shadow of
## the End of the World?

There is an increasing awareness in Evangelical Christianity of the tremendous redemptive-eschatological significance of the fall of Jerusalem in AD 70. That event is no longer being seen as simply the destruction of the Jewish capital, no matter how awful or gruesome the physical event was. It is becoming more and more clear that the fall of that city had tremendous *spiritual* importance.

Noted scholar R. C. Sproul has written: "No matter what view of eschatology we embrace, we must take seriously the redemptive-historical importance of Jerusalem's destruction in A.D.70."[1]

Kenneth Gentry writes of AD 70, "God is preparing to punish His people Israel, remove the temple system, and re-orient redemptive history from one people and land to all peoples throughout the earth (Matthew 8:10-11; 21:43; John 4:23). This dramatic redemptive-historical event not only ends the Old Covenant era, but points to the end of history itself."[2] He says in another place, "The significance of the collapse of Jerusalem and the destruction of the temple in AD 70 is little appreciated by modern Christians. But, AD 70 effectively closes out the old, typological era and removes a major hindrance to the spread of the Christian faith."[3]

We could multiply such quotes. Even in circles of higher academia, the meaning of Jerusalem's demise is being expressed. N. T. Wright, one of the leading Jesus Scholars of the day, said this of the cataclysmic events of AD 70:

> "It is uncontroversial to point out that this (1 Thessalonians 4:13f, DKP), is Paul's reworking of

[1] R. C. Sproul, *The Last Days According to Jesus,* (Grand Rapids, Baker, 1998)26.

[2] Kenneth Gentry, *He Shall Have Dominion,* (Draper, VA., 2009)342.

[3] Kenneth Gentry, *The Great Tribulation: Past or Future. Two Evangelicals Debate the Question*, (Grand Rapids, Kregel, 1999)64.

the Jewish 'Day of the Lord' traditions; but it is highly controversial to point out, as I did...that for Paul, 'the Day of the Lord' by no means denoted the end of the world. Just as in Amos or Jeremiah the really appalling thing about the Day of YHWH was that there would be another day after it–had it been the actual end of the world it would have been a shame, but there wouldn't have been anybody around to worry about it after it had happened–so in Paul the Day of the Lord is clearly something which might well happen during the continuing lifetimes of himself and his readers. It is something you might hear about in a letter. Nevertheless, it is a great moment of judgment as a result of which everything will be different, and the world will be changed. ...I have no hesitation in saying that, had Paul been alive in the year we call AD 70, when the convulsions in Rome during the Year of the Four Emperors were quickly followed by the destruction of Jerusalem, he would have said, 'That's it. That's the Day of the Lord.' I think that this is precisely what the notorious passage in 1 Thessalonians 2:16 is referring to; God's wrath has come upon them *eis telos*, in a climactic and decisive way."[4]

Wright cites Sanders in regard to the Temple and its place in the mind of Israel: "I think that it is almost impossible to make too much of the Temple in first century Jewish Palestine."[5] Anderson noted that: "No greater cultic calamity could be imagined than the loss of this sacrifice, (the Temple cultus, DKP), since it symbolized the severing of the divine-human relationship (Daniel 8:11)." (Cited in Wright, *Victory*, 407, n. 133).

---

[4] N. T. Wright, *Paul*, (Minneapolis, Fortress, 2005)141.

[5] N. T. Wright, *Jesus and the Victory of God*, (Minneapolis, Fortress, 1996)406f.

In spite of this growing awareness and appreciation of the events of AD 70, it is increasingly common in some circles today, especially in the Amillennial and Postmillennial world, to claim that the end of the age judgment in AD 70 was a type of the real "end of the world." This idea has become increasingly popular since the advocates of Covenant Eschatology[6] began emphasizing that AD 70 was the fulfillment of all things written (Luke 21:22).

It is my personal opinion that the claim that AD 70 was typological of the "real" end of the age has become so popular among amillennialists and postmillennialists because the Biblical testimony is so patently clear that the end of the age, the coming of the Lord, and the Great Assize, truly was near in the first century. However, to (ostensibly) honor the imminence language and yet maintain a futurist eschatology, it is claimed that while AD 70 was indeed historically- redemptively significant, as the turning point of the ages, it was in fact a mere shadow, or type of the true end, the end of time and human history.

I want to address and dispel the idea that AD 70 was a foreshadowing of the end of human history. This book is an expansion of material that I presented in my book *Like Father Like Son, On Clouds of Glory.*[7] There, I presented five reasons for rejecting this idea. I will increase that in this work, although even then, I will not have by any means exhausted all of the reasons for rejecting the idea.

---

[6] Covenant Eschatology is also called full preterism, "realized eschatology", and other terms, some pejorative of course, such as "hyper-preterists" coined by Postmillennialists. I personally do not care much for the term "preterist" since it carries a lot of negative "baggage." The term Covenant Eschatology is far more accurate, since it defines Biblical eschatology as the end of the Old Covenant age of Israel– i.e. AD 70– and not "historical eschatology" i.e. the end of time and human history.

[7] Don K. Preston, *Like Father Like Son, On Clouds of Glory,* (Ardmore, Ok. JaDon Productions, 2010).

Since I presented the material in that book I have come to realize that it is not overstating the case to say the idea of AD 70 being a type of a future eschaton is a foundational, critical tenet of these two schools, particularly the Postmillennialists.

Postmillennial apologist Kenneth Gentry commenting on Matthew 24 says: "Theologically, a redemptive-historical link does in fact connect AD 70 with the second advent. This could easily confuse the disciples. That is, the AD 70 episode is an anticipatory foreshadowing of the larger event, the second advent."[8] In another place, he says: "I wholeheartedly concur that A.D. 70 and the destruction of the temple is a 'proleptic, typological fulfillment of the final judgment.'"[9] He says that Revelation 19 is A.D. 70 but is typological of the end of time. Gentry was responding to Strimple.

Gary North says just as there was a Great Tribulation resulting from the loosing of Satan in the first century, "The devil will be loosed for a little season at the end of time, meaning his power over the nations returns to him in full strength (Rev. 20:3).[10]

Not all Dominionists agree. Keith Mathison categorically rejects North's view: "There is no end time tribulation. Jesus' prophecy about tribulation in Matthew 24 was fulfilled between AD 30 and AD 70."[11] Contrast Mathison with Amillennialist Kim Riddlebarger immediately below, who clearly does believe that the Great Tribulation and anti-christ of the first century were typological of a future Tribulation and anti-christ.

---

[8] Kenneth Gentry, *Revelation Made Easy*, (Powder Springs, GA, 2009)47.

[9] *Thine Is the Kingdom*, (Vallecito, Ca., Chalcedon, 2003)159f.

[10] Gary North, *Dominion* and Common Grace, (Tyler, Tx. Institute for Christian Economics, 1987)170.

[11] Keith Mathison, *Dispensationalism: Rightly Dividing the House of God?*, (Philippsburg, NJ, 1995)144.

4

Amillennialist Kim Riddlebarger agrees that AD 70 was a foreshadowing of the "real" end of the age, i.e. the end of time and history, when he says: "In the context of predictive prophecy and prophetic perspective, the intent would be that the destruction of the temple and the tribulation brought by the Roman army is a type of greater wrath experienced immediately before the return of Christ, perhaps connected with the loosing of Satan (Revelation 20:7f) and this on a global, not a local scale. This means that Jerusalem and the temple are, perhaps, a type of the apostate church in the last days."[12] He also says: "Christ has fulfilled the Old Testament promises regarding the coming of the messianic age. The prospect of a future kingdom indicates that Christ's fulfillment of these Old Testament promises is typological of a more glorious and final kingdom yet to come" (2003,113).

Noted Amillennialist Greg Beale concurs with Riddlebarger: "The events of AD 70 point typologically to the events at the very end of the world."[13] Likewise, popular radio host Hank Hanegraaff says: "the destruction of Jerusalem in AD 70 and the prophecies thereof serve as types that at once point forward to and guarantee a day of ultimate judgment when Christ will appear a second time to judge the living and the dead."[14]

Notice Riddlebarger's emphasis on the fulfillment of the Old Covenant types / prophecies, and the creation of a brand new set of promises (in reality a *new eschatology*) which are now the types and shadows of a yet future eschaton. In fact, Riddlebarger says : "Because of Jesus Christ and his coming, the Christian possesses the complete," notice his wording here, "the complete fulfillment and blessings of all of the promises of the messianic age named under the Old Covenant.

---

[12] *A Case for Amillennialism*, (Grand Rapids, Baker Academic,2003)262, n. 34.

[13] Greg Beale, *The Temple and the Church's Mission*, (Downer's Grove, InterVarsity, 2004)213, n. 29.

[14] Hank Hanegraaff, *Apocalypse Code*, (Nashville, Nelson, 2007)257, n. 75.

But the arrival of the messianic age also brought with it a new series of promises to be fulfilled at the end of the age." (2003,262, n. 34).

So, Beale, Riddlebarger, Hanegraaff et. al, see the end of the Old Covenant age in AD 70 as a foreshadowing and type of the end of the Christian age. As we shall see, this is hugely problematic for these men. They are in fact, creating an eschatology unknown in scripture, by insisting the Old Testament types are fulfilled, but that Christ has given us a new set of (types and shadows) promises, of another end, the real end.

Dispensationalists do not often speak of AD 70 being typological of the real end. In fact, many Dispensationalists, in contrast to Amillennialists and Postmillennialists, seem loathe to even admit the significance of AD 70 in any way. There are exceptions, however.

For instance, Thomas Ice, with whom I have had four debates,[15] says this of the fall of Jerusalem as described in Luke 21:22 "Those first century days are called the 'days of vengeance' for Jerusalem is under the divine judgment of covenantal sanctions recorded in Leviticus 26 and Deuteronomy 28. Luke notes that God's vengeance on His elect nation 'is in order that all things that are written may be fulfilled.' Jesus is telling the nation that God will fulfill all the curses of the Mosaic Covenant because of Israel's disobedience. He will not relent and merely bring to pass a partial fulfillment of His vengeance. Some of the passages that Jesus says will be fulfilled include the following: Leviticus 26:27-33; Deuteronomy 28:49-63; Deuteronomy 32:19-27; 1 Kings 9:1-9; Jeremiah 6:1-6; 26:1-9; Daniel 9:26; Hosea 8:1-10:15; Micah 3:12; Zechariah 11:6."[16]

---

[15] DVDs of one formal public debate with Ice are available from me via my websites: www.eschatology.org, or www.bibleprophecy.com.

[16] Thomas Ice and Kenneth Gentry, *The Great Tribulation, Past or Future?* A Formal Written Debate, ( Grand Rapids, Kregel,1999) 98.

It is difficult to see how anyone could affirm the total fulfillment of the prophecies that Ice cites and yet affirm the Dispensational view. Notice his insistence that the AD 70 judgment was not "partial" but that "all the curses of the Mosaic Covenant" were completely fulfilled. Well, if the AD 70 judgment was not partial, but completely fulfilled all the Covenantal Curses of Torah, then it was patently not typological, or a foreshadowing of another, fuller, more complete fulfillment.

While Dispensationalists do not emphasize AD 70 as *typological* of the end of the Christian age, they do, however, employ a hermeneutic that lends itself to that perspective. And in reality, they do occasionally use the term foreshadowing and similar terms. They most often employ the principle of the "Double Fulfillment of Prophecy." In other words, ancient prophecies may have had an imminent fulfillment to satisfy the language of "audience relevance" but, those prophecies will be ultimately fulfilled again, in the last days.

Interestingly enough, when the postmillennialists– *who affirm that AD 70 was typological*-- are writing or speaking against Dispensationalists, they condemn the idea that first century events typify future events.

Kenneth Gentry, attacking the Dispensational paradigm, says, "There are those, moved by the strong arguments for a preteristic understanding of Revelation, who hold there is still a beast in our future. The means by which they attempt this is through 'double fulfillment.' These interpreters argue that though there is a past fulfillment of the beast, there will nevertheless be another climactic fulfillment in the future. Such an approach to the beast of Revelation is highly unlikely."[17]

Gentry proceeded to give three reasons why he rejects the Double Fulfillment paradigm, and we will examine his reasons (all excellent)

---

[17] Kenneth Gentry, *Perilous Times, A Study In Eschatological Evil,* (Texarkana, Covenant Media Press, 1999)133.

as we proceed. But, Gentry is not alone in rejecting the Double Fulfillment concept.

At the 2011 Prophecy Conference sponsored by American Vision, Joel McDurmon, Head of Research at American Vision, presented a speech entitled "Double Fulfillment: Double Cross." In that presentation he examined the Dispensational claim that Bible prophecy must be fulfilled twice. Thus, as noted just above, Dispensationalists claim that while many OT prophecies– and some New Testament ones-- did have "audience relevance" for the ancient audiences to whom they were addressed, those prophecies will be fulfilled again in the last days. McDurmon categorically rejected this hermeneutic.

Then, in his book, *Jesus –V- Jerusalem* (which is excellent in many ways) McDurmon, attacked the Dispensational "double fulfillment" practice, especially as it relates to the anti-christ. Millennialists claim that the first century "anti-christs" that John spoke of in 1 John 2:18 as already present—in fulfillment of prophecy, by the way-- "prefigure" the "final, greater" end times anti-christ. McDurmon said this double fulfillment practice "distorts the scripture."[18]

However, in 2012, I had a formal public debate with McDurmon.[19] And strangely enough, McDurmon took the position that prophecy is not only fulfilled twice, but, it is fulfilled over and over again, "multiple times." It seems that Double Fulfillment is only wrong when the Dispensationalists appeal to it, but, it is in truth *critical* to the Postmillennial (Dominionist) eschatology and theology. Let me illustrate.

---

[18] Joel McDurmon, *Jesus -v-Jerusalem*, (Powder Springs, GA., American Vision, 2011)185.

[19] DVDs and MP3s of that debate are available at www.bibleprophecy.com, or, www.eschatology.org. As I write this the MSS of that debate is at the proof reader as well, and should be published shortly.

During our debate, McDurmon actually admitted that he could freely posit fulfillment of 1 Corinthians 15 and Revelation 20 (the resurrection, destruction of the "last enemy", White Throne Judgment at the end of the millennium, etc.) in AD 70. *That is not a typo.* McDurmon openly affirmed that there was "a fulfillment" of these texts (owing to the fact that they contain language of imminence) but that we still await the "final fulfillment."

Very clearly, then, if the "AD 70 was a type of the real end" hermeneutic is invalid and unscriptural, then Amillennialism and Postmillennialism– not to mention Dispensationalism-- are falsified. You cannot logically affirm the AD 70 fulfillment of 1 Corinthians 15 and Revelation 20 and yet posit another end, another fulfillment, if AD 70 was not typological.

In fact, some Postmillennialists, at least when writing against the Double Fulfillment hermeneutic, seem to reject McDurmon's multiple fulfillment hermeneutic.

Noted Postmillennialist Lorraine Boettner says: "Another principle of interpretation is that when a prophecy or promise has been fulfilled once, there is no valid reason why it must be fulfilled again, or repeatedly."[20]

Kenneth Gentry, outspoken apologist for Postmillennialism, likewise (ostensibly) condemns the premillennial appeal to Double Fulfillment.

Responding to millennialist Marvin Pate, who argued that the anti-christs of 1 John 2:18 are predictive of the ultimate, final anti-christ, Gentry says: "Pate specifically notes that the mark of the beast 'can be

---

[20] Lorraine Boettner in, *The Meaning of the Millennium, Four Views*, edited by Robert Clouse, (Downers Grove, Ill., Intervarsity Press, 1977)105. Of course, it may well be that Boettner was inconsistent and while rejecting the double fulfillment practice nonetheless believed that AD 70 was typological. I have not discovered that yet, but, it is common among postmillennialists, as we are seeing.

understood as pointing a guilty finger at those Jews in the first century.' Why, then, should we look for further fulfillments beyond this most relevant first century one?"[21]

So, on the one hand, Dominionists condemn as untenable the Dispensational theorem of prophetic "Double Fulfillment." It is unscriptural, unwarranted and false. However, those same Postmillennialists insist not only on Double Fulfillment, but on many, *multiple fulfillments!*

Significantly, the early church seemed to have no concept of the view that AD 70- or first century events– were typological of future literal events. On the contrary, they believed that they were the fulfillment of those Old Covenant types. They believed– at least some of them– that the age of types and shadows came to an end in AD 70.

Athanasius (fourth century) said: "Now observe; that city, since the coming of our Savior, has had an end, and all the land of the Jews has been laid waste; so that from the testimony of these things (and we need' no further proof, being assured by our own eyes of the fact) there must, of necessity, be an end of the shadow" (Festal Letters, VIII).

Athanasius certainly did not ascribe to the Dominionist hermeneutic of multiple fulfillments of prophecy.

The early fathers also believed that the Old Covenant types were literal and physical, while their fulfillment was strictly spiritual.[22]

Theoderet of Cyrus speaking against the Jews said, "Let them show us their Jerusalem delivered from tears. For that city (Jewish Jerusalem)

---

[21] Kenneth Gentry, *Four Views of Revelation*, (Grand Rapids, Zondervan, 1998)45.

[22] Robert Wilken, *The Land Called Holy, Palestine In Christian History and Thought*, (New Haven, Yale University Press, 1992)325, n. 11, has a great discussion of this.

10

was handed over to many misfortunes, whereas for this city (the heavenly Jerusalem) alone enjoys life without grief and free of tears." (Commenting on Isaiah 65:19 and cited in Guinot, 3:324).[23]

Very clearly then, at least some prominent members of the early church believed that the fulfillment of the Old Covenant physical realities had been fulfilled spiritually in Christ.

This is in stark contrast to the modern Dominionist view,[24] expressed in my debate with McDurmon.[25] He agreed that the Old Covenant types were literal, and foreshadowed New Covenant, spiritual realities,[26] but then insisted that the New Covenant spiritual realities

---

[23] Cited by Wilken in *The Land Called Holy*, (324, n. 1 of chapter 11 heading).

[24] Of course, it is humorous to hear and read the modern Postmillennialists take positions that are so blatantly out of step with ancient Christian belief, for no one likes to point to the historical view of the church more than the Dominionists! Gentry, Mathison, McDurmon, et. al. love to castigate advocates of Covenant Eschatology because that doctrine is not "historical" or "creedal." And yet, these same men are, increasingly, taking more and more positions that are simply not found in church history or in the creeds! See my *The Elements Shall Melt With Fervent Heat*, where I discuss this self contradiction within the Postmillennial world.

[25] The late Greg Bahnsen, noted apologist for the Dominionist movement, affirmed that the typological seventh day Sabbath of Torah has been abrogated. We now have the "Christian Sabbath" which is typological of a another, "real," future Sabbath! Greg Bahnsen, *Theonomy in Christian Ethics*, (Nagadoches, Tx., Covenant Media Press, 2002)226.

[26] During the debate I produced a chart from McDurmon's writings (writing against Dispensationalists), in which the millennialists focused on the literal, physical nature of the Zion promises. McDurmon categorically rejected those claims, and insisted that "all of the promises concerning Zion have been spiritualized and fulfilled in Christ." The chart was

now foreshadow coming literal, physical realities. I repeatedly challenged McDurmon to exegetically justify this claim, but he never attempted to provide that.

Our point here is that it is clearly self contradictory for the Dominionist to decry the validity of the Dispensational view of double fulfillment of prophecy, and then turn around and *insist* on the *multiple* fulfillment of prophecy. If there is no scriptural warrant for saying that the first century anti-christs foreshadowed a future anti-christ, then there is no justification for claiming that the end of the age in AD 70 foreshadows another end of the age– i.e. the end of time.

I think you can see from what we have seen thus far that it is *critically important* to the various futurist eschatologies to demonstrate that AD 70 was a type or foreshadowing of a future end of the age. However, we have the right to demand some solid exegetical demonstration that this is true. But I will be blunt here. I have not seen a shred of *textual, exegetical evidence* offered by any of the men cited above to support that hermeneutic. All I have seen are bold assertions that this is the case. Notice the quotes given above, and take note of the *conspicuous absence* of any attempt at scriptural justification for their claims.

Now, if the futurist schools cannot prove with solid exegetical support, that the events of AD 70 were typological of another true end of the age, then in reality, all futurist eschatologies fail. If AD 70 was not a foreshadowing of another eschaton, then the AD 70 parousia and end of the age must have been the "real one."

There is no doubt whatsoever that the NT writers affirmed the nearness of "the end", "the end of the age", "the parousia", even the resurrection.[27] Furthermore, there is no textual support for the idea that

clearly troublesome to McDurmon, and he never offered any kind of substantive response. DVDs of the debate are available from my websites.

[27] See my *Can God Tell Time?* for a full discussion of the time statements in the NT, and a refutation of the attempts to negate those statements. Available from my websites.

they looked beyond the eschatological events that they said were near, to another Day of the Lord that was not near.

So, the question might be asked: Why all the emphasis on the claim that AD 70 was typological? Why deny that AD 70 was the consummation? The answer is simple: It is because of the futurist view of protology, the story of the beginning, the story of Eden.

All futurist views believe that the death introduced through the sin of Adam was physical death. They likewise believe that physical creation was cursed at that time, but that we are waiting for the literal, physical restoration of planet earth.[28] Romans 8 is one of the keys to this theology, but I clearly do not have space to develop it here.

The point is that since all three futurist views believe that physical death is the death introduced by Adam, and that there must be a physical resurrection of human corpses at the end of human history.[29] I am not going to discuss the nature of the death of Adam or of the resurrection here.

---

[28] In the Amillennial tradition of my youth, this doctrine was troublesome to say the least. On the one hand it was affirmed that we are waiting on the restoration of all things. On the other hand it was taught that we are waiting for the end of time and *the elemental destruction of the physical cosmos.* It was never explained how the destruction of the universe could be the restoration of the Garden! At numerous lectureship open forums that I attended, this issue was clearly a thorn in the flesh.

[29] See my *We Shall Meet Him In The Air, the Wedding of the King of kings,* for an extensive discussion of the nature of the death introduced by Adam. Simply stated, there is no support for the idea that Adam introduced biological death into the world. And this fact changes the entire story of eschatology. The book is available on my websites, on Kindle, Amazon and other retailers.

However, with this being said, if I am able to demonstrate that the idea of AD 70 being typological is false, I will have totally undermined the futurist eschatologies and their view of Adamic death. That is how important this study is. If AD 70 was not typological of a yet future end of the world, then the end of the age, consummating the last days, arrived in AD 70, and there is no end of time in our future. I believe that my case can be and will be established beyond dispute.

So, we want now to present several reason why AD 70 was not, and could not be, a type or shadow of the "real" end.

> **If AD 70 was not a typological foreshadowing of the "real" end, the futurist concepts about Adam, the Curse and Death are all falsified.**
> **The NT writers all affirm the imminence of the end of the age, the judgment, the destruction of Satan, the parousia and the resurrection. So, if the events they anticipated were near, and were not typological, then they were expecting the consummation of the eschatological schema– and there is not another judgment, another parousia, another resurrection, another end of the age.**

> **Reason #1 - The Old Testament prophets never foretold two ends of two ages, two kingdoms, two resurrections or two last days.**

The New Testament writers are adamant in repeatedly affirming that their eschatological hope was nothing other than the OT promises made to Israel.[30] Paul said his doctrine of the resurrection was found in Moses, the Law and the prophets (Acts 24:14-15). He preached nothing but the hope of Israel found in Moses and the prophets (Acts 26:21f), and said he was on trial for preaching the hope of Israel (Acts 28).

Peter likewise said that his proclamation of the "restoration of all things" to be completed at Christ's parousia was foretold by "all the prophets who have ever spoken" (Acts 3:23f). His expectation of the Day of the Lord to bring in the New Creation was promised by the prophets of old (2 Peter 3:1-2, 13).

Even in the Apocalypse, the apostles anticipated the resurrection at the sounding of the seventh trumpet, the time of the resurrection, and said this would be when the mystery of God foretold by the prophets would be finished (Revelation 10:7).

What is so critical about all of this is that in the Old Testament, we do not find the prediction of two eschatons. I will not take the time to document this extensively, as that would take us too far afield. But take note of just a few examples:

---

[30] See my *We Shall Meet Him In The Air* for full documentation of this critical fact. It is one of the most ignored, but most critical facts in the entire study of eschatology.

15

1.) Isaiah foretold the last days establishment of the kingdom and Messianic Temple (Isaiah 2-4). Those last days would be a time of famine and warfare when the people of Jerusalem would die from famine and the sword (Isaiah 3:13-24). That time would be climaxed by the Day of the Lord when He would avenge the blood guilt of Jerusalem by the spirit of judgment and fire (Isaiah 4:4f), and then establish the promised sanctuary.

2.) The OT foretold the "Wedding" of Messiah at his coming (Isaiah 62). This is of course one of Jesus' favorite themes, not to mention the Apocalypse. Jesus emphatically posited the Wedding at the judgment and destruction of Jerusalem (Matthew 22:1f).

3.) The OT prophets foretold the resurrection, and it would be "when the power of the holy people is completely shattered" (Daniel 12:2-7). It would likewise be when Leviathan, i.e. the Devil, would be destroyed. This is patently the prediction of the end of the millennium resurrection of Revelation 20. But, Isaiah is clear that this would be when YHVH would cast off the people He had created, and turn the "fortified city" into a wilderness, and turn the altar into chalkstone (Isaiah 25-27).

4.) Isaiah foretold the New Heaven and Earth where righteousness would dwell, and emphatically placed its arrival after "the Lord God shall slay you" (Isaiah 65:13f).

Any reader of those prophecies knows those prophets never looked beyond that which they predicted to something else, something better. There is one end times hope, one end times scenario.

It is interesting and significant that some of the most vocal adversaries of Covenant Eschatology admit that the OT never anticipated another eschaton beyond Israel's last days. As I point out in my book, *We*

*Shall Meet Him In The Air, the Wedding of the King of kings,*[31] Gentry says:

> "From the linear perspective of the Old Testament, ancient Israel believes that the "age to come' will be the Messianic era *that would fully arrive after their current age ends.* Yet in the New Testament we learn that the 'age to come' begins in principle with the first century coming of Christ. It overlaps with 'this age' which begins in Christ." Thus, we are not only children of 'this age' (present, sin-laden temporal history), but are also spiritually children of 'the age to come' (the final, perfected eternal age). We have our feet in both worlds" (*Dominion*, 2009, 326, my emphasis).

This is really quite stunning for it admits that the OT prophets did not teach that AD 70 was typological of anything! It admits that what the OT prophets foretold was the full arrival of the New Creation, not at the end of human history, and not at the end of the Christian age. They predicted the consummation at the end of the Mosaic age.

It is to be noted that some leading reformed amillennialists have inadvertently "given the farm away" when it comes to the solution to the Adamic Curse and AD 70.

In 2003 I had a formal debate with James Jordan.[32] He actually argued that the Adamic Curse was resolved in AD 70! He is on record

---

[31] This book is, to my knowledge, the first and only full preterist (fulfilled) commentary on 1 Thessalonians 4:13f that has been produced. It has been called a systematic theology by some reviewers. It can be purchased from Amazon, my websites and other retailers.

[32] DVDs and a book of my debate with Jordan are available from my websites, Kindle, Amazon and other retailers.

saying: "The World of Genesis 2-3 ended in A.D. 70"[33] However, he then tried to delineate between the final solution of the Adamic Curse and the eschatological promises to Israel. In response, I noted that in 1 Corinthians 15 Paul conflates the Adamic Curse with Israel's promises, positing fulfillment at the end of Torah. This clearly stunned Jordan, as he admitted in private conversation afterward.

It needs to be understood very clearly that if the OT prophets foretold the full arrival of the New Creation at the end of the Mosaic age, (something Jordan, Gentry, DeMar, McDurmon all seem to say) then any suggestion that AD 70 was typological of anything yet to come is wrong.

We could document all of this even more, but this will suffice to prove the point. What is so critical to grasp is that what those prophets anticipated is indubitably what the NT writers longed for.

The NT writers tell us that their hope of the "restoration of all things," the "time of reformation," the New Creation, the resurrection and parousia, was nothing but the hope of Israel, promised in Torah. And, this is significant, they tell us that there was but *one hope* (Ephesians 4:4)[34] While they tells us repeatedly that they anticipated the solution to the Adamic Curse, they posit that fulfillment at the end of Torah, not at the end of time[35]. This amounts to *prima facie*

---

[33] The quote is found on tape # 1 and 4 of a series Jordan did on the issue of preterism."The A.D. 70 Question," 1986).

[34] In my 2012 formal debate with Joel McDurmon, I emphasized this "one hope" concept, and demonstrated that the "one hope" was nothing but the hope of Old Covenant Israel, found in the Old Testament. McDurmon tried desperately to find an eschatology, a resurrection, divorced from Israel's promises, but, of course, he could not do it. DVDs of that debate are available from my websites.

[35] In the debate just mentioned, I demonstrated from Hebrews 11 that the hope of the "better resurrection"

refutation of the idea that the events of the first century typified other eschatological events.

In other words, the OT prophets foretold one eschaton. The NT writers said their eschatological hope was that foretold by the prophets of old, and, they said there was but *one hope*. So, if there is an eschatological hope different from and beyond that foretold by the Old Covenant prophets, then we have no record of it, and no way to prove it.

Let me put it like this: The OT prophets anticipated the Day of the Lord, the resurrection and the New Creation. They said those wonderful blessings would arrive at the time of the passing of the Old Covenant world of Israel, when that old world would be shattered and destroyed. The New Testament writers all say that they were living in the prophesied days, and were anticipating what the Old Covenant prophets predicted. And yet, we are told today that we should be looking for the end of human history, the end of the Christian age, the end of the New Covenant world!

If this is so, then there were / are two hopes in scripture. But this clearly violates what the Bible says. There was but one hope, and that hope was what the OT prophets foretold, to be fulfilled at the end of the Old Covenant world. The creation of a "New Testament" eschatology, positing the end of the New Covenant creation is, to reiterate, the creation of another hope, the creation of *two* hopes.

Biblically, there was but one true eschatological hope, and that one hope was focused on the end of the Old Covenant age in AD 70.[36]

---

(Hebrews 11:35) anticipated by all of the OT worthies, extended from Abel, to Enoch, to Noah, to Abraham, and to Moses, culminating in Zion, which, prophetically is the locus of the resurrection (Isaiah 25:6f).

[36] I emphasized this indisputable fact repeatedly in my debate with McDurmon. Postmillennialists like to affirm a "Jewish eschaton" but say it was not the real one. The real story of eschatology is Adamic, or even Abrahamic, they tell us, ignoring the fact that in the NT the Adamic / Abrahamic

Thus, the suggestion that AD 70 was a foreshadowing of a greater, true eschaton is clearly misguided, and without textual warrant.[37]

Our first point is established then. The OT prophets never foretold two eschatologies, two last days, two resurrections. Their one hope was to be fulfilled at the end of the Old Covenant age, in AD 70. Thus, AD 70 was not a type of foreshadowing of another last days, another end of the age, another eschaton.

---

eschatology is conflated into the story of Israel, and fulfillment is posited at the end of Torah. The undeniable reality of this "one hope" was hugely problematic for Joel– and all Dominionists.

[37] An additional, critical supporting fact is that not only do the NT prophets say there was but one hope, the hope of Israel found in Torah, but, they tell us repeatedly that they were living in the days foretold by those OT prophets (cf. Matthew 13:17; Acts 3:23-24; 1 Peter 1:10-12) and that the consummation was near (1 Peter 4:5-17). I will not take the time here to develop this further, but, it is a vital supportive tenet of what we have just presented. The NT writers simply never looked beyond their days to another last days, another eschaton. Thus, the imminent fulfillment that they anticipated, was not typological of anything.

20

> **Reason #2 - The Christian age has no end. Thus, the end of the Old Covenant age could not be typological of the end of that which is endless!**

As just seen, the Old Covenant prophets anticipated the end of the Mosaic Covenant age. They never predicted the end of time, or the end of the Christian age. And yet, fundamental to all evangelical eschatology is the idea that the current Christian age is destined to come to a cataclysmic end.

Let me set before the reader in the simplest form possible, the dilemma faced by all three futurist schools of eschatology:

**The Day of the Lord, judgment and resurrection occur at the end of the age.**

**But, the Christian age has no end.**

**Therefore, the Day of the Lord, judgment and resurrection do not occur at the end of the Christian age.**

Several OT prophecies speak of the unending nature of the Messianic kingdom.

Psalms 89:34f says that the throne of Messiah would be established forever, and as firmly as the sun, moon and stars.[38] To the ancients, the

---

[38] I am, naturally, well aware of the OT language that depicts the Day of the Lord as the dissolution of the "sun, moon and stars." See my *The Elements Shall Melt With Fervent Heat* book, in which I demonstrate that this language is metaphoric, describing in highly exaggerated manner, the downfall of ancient societies or kingdoms. It is becoming increasingly common in the scholarly world to recognize that

physical cosmos was the most firmly fixed, unmoving, permanent thing they knew. Other things, almost everything, passed away, but the creation remained firm (Ecclesiastes 1:4). In fact, the firmness of the physical creation is tied to the glory of God's existence in Psalms 72.

Isaiah 9:6-9 speaks of Messiah's kingdom and *evangelism* into the kingdom as being "without end." This is a simple, yet profoundly important statement of fact. If evangelism never ends, the Christian age never ends, and that alone falsifies the idea that AD 70 foreshadowed the end of the Christian age.

Notice how this agrees with Revelation 21-22. After the "end" of Revelation 20, i.e. the resurrection and judgment, we find that there are still nations outside the city. There are also "dogs, liars and those who work abomination" (21:27; 22:15). Inside the city is the tree of life that produces its fruit *twelve months a year*, which challenges rather strongly the idea of "the end of time." But, the fruit of that tree is for "the healing of the nations" (Revelation 22:3-4). Here is ongoing evangelism after the end.[39]

Of course, in most circles it is common to read that Christ *surrenders his throne* at the parousia. It is argued that the *kingdom* is eternal, but Christ's rule over the kingdom ends at his coming when he "delivers the kingdom to the Father" (1 Corinthians 15:24). Jesus supposedly abdicates his throne at his coming.

Wayne Jackson, outspoken critic of Covenant Eschatology wrote: "Now, remember that according to verse 24, when He comes again, He

---

the ancient Jews, and those in Jesus' day, neither had a concept of the "end of time" nor expected that to occur at the Day of the Lord.

[39] There is a great deal more here. In this post judgment world, sons of God are being produced (cf. Luke 20)– see Revelation 21:7. See my three part series "Children From Stones:"
http://www.bibleprophecy.com/children-from-stones-the-callin g-of-abraham-and-his-seed/#more-%27.

will no longer be reigning, because He will have delivered the kingdom back to the Father."[40] Similarly, in several formal debates, my Amillennial and Postmillennial opponents have made the identical arguments. But, this idea is badly mistaken.

At his coming, Christ would *sit* on the throne, *not quit the throne* (Matthew 25:31f). This surely does not sound like an abdication of kingdom authority.

Notice the following as well:

Christ was on the throne of David prior to the parousia, (Psalms 110; Acts 2; Acts 13). That period of time must be seen as the time when he was "consolidating" his rule and authority. See Luke 19 and the parable of the man who went into the far country to receive his kingdom.[41] The parousia is the time when his last enemy, death, per 1 Corinthians 15 would be conquered. So, the question is, does the king abdicate his rule and throne when he has successfully put down his enemies, or, does he in fact enter into the full reign?

The parousia of Christ is the time of his Wedding. Much more on this theme later, but note the following:

**The parousia of Matthew 25:31f is the coming of Matthew 25:1-14– Christ's coming for the Wedding.**

---

[40] Wayne Jackson– *The AD 70 Theory: A Review of the Max King Doctrine*, (Stockton, CA., Courier Publications,1990)37. Jackson's book is one of the most illogical, desperate attempts to address Covenant Eschatology imaginable. Misrepresentations, faulty logic and self-contradictions abound.

[41] Observe that the man went into the far country to receive his kingdom and returns *to rule over that kingdom*, not to abdicate from the throne he had been given!

23

**But, the Wedding would occur at the fall of Jerusalem– Matthew 22:1-10.[42]**

**Therefore, the coming of the Lord in Matthew 25:31 occurred at the fall of Jerusalem.**

Now, Jackson and many commentators insist that *paradidoi* in 1 Corinthians 15:24 (translated as "deliver") must mean surrender; it can't mean *share*.[43] Well, let's look at the Wedding motif again:

**Christ's Coming in Matthew 25:31F; 1 Corinthians 15; 1 Thessalonians 4, Revelation 19, etc. Is When He Surrenders, Abdicates, His Rule over the Kingdom, Giving it to the Father, according to virtually all futurist paradigms.**

**But, the Coming in Matthew 25, Corinthians, Rev. 19, Etc. Is the Time of Christ's Wedding.**

**Therefore, at His Coming for His Wedding, Christ Divorces His Wife. He Hands Her over to the Father And Is No Longer Married to Her.**

The view that Christ surrenders his bride at the parousia flies in the face of what Paul said in Ephesians 5:25f. Christ would *present the church to himself* (Ephesians 5). I have consulted over 50 commentators, and everyone of them agrees: *the presentation occurs at the parousia.*

---

[42] See my *We Shall Meet Him In The Air, The Wedding of the King of kings*, for a full exposition and discussion of Matthew 22 and the Wedding motif. The book is available from Amazon, my websites, and other retailers.

[43] Those who make this argument conveniently overlook the fact that Paul uses the identical word in v. 1-2 to say that he had delivered the gospel to the Corinthians. Very clearly, Paul did not surrender his authority over the gospel; he *shared* the gospel with them.

So, if AD 70 was the presentation of the church to Christ at his Wedding,[44] then the idea of the end of the Christian age, the abdication of the throne by Jesus is simply wrong.[45]

If the Wedding was in AD 70, as most Dominionists and some Amillennialists agree, then any idea of an abdication of the throne by Jesus is wrong. You can't have abdication and presentation all occurring at the same moment. This is supported by the fact that scripture posits Christ on the throne with the Father, *after the end.* Notice two quick verses;

➡ Revelation 11:15-18 –

"Then the seventh angel sounded: And there were loud voices in heaven, saying, "The kingdoms of this world have become the kingdoms of our Lord and of His Christ, and He shall reign forever and ever!"And the twenty-four elders who sat before God on their thrones fell on their faces and worshiped God, 17 saying: "We give You thanks, O Lord God Almighty, The One who is and who was and who is to come, Because You have taken Your great power and reigned. The nations were angry, and Your wrath has come, And the time of the dead, that they should be judged, And that You should reward Your servants the prophets and the saints, And those who fear Your name, small and great, And should destroy those who destroy the earth."

---

[44] More about the Wedding issue below.

[45] In numerous written debates my Amillennial opponents have argued for the abdication of the throne by Jesus. However, when I have shown that even they posit Christ's wedding at his parousia, thus demanding that the church be "presented" to him (and not divorced), there has been total silence in response. You cannot have Christ divorcing the Bride at the very moment of his wedding, can you?

There are several things to observe here:
It is the time of the resurrection.
It is the time of the seventh, i.e. the last trump of 1 Corinthians 15, *when Christ supposedly abdicates the throne.*
This all takes place at the time of the destruction of the city, "where the Lord was slain" (11:8).
It is the time when the Father and the Son, enter fully into the kingdom reign, and *"they"* not just the Father, but *they*, then rule "for ever and for ever," *together.*

Beale, commenting on Revelation 19 says the Greek term translated forever and forever, as in chapter 11, "refers to an unending period as throughout the book."[46]

So, we have the time of the resurrection and the kingdom, the time when Christ *supposedly* hands over the kingdom, surrendering his kingly authority. Yet, in Revelation there is no such concept. There is no surrendering of the throne. There is no abdication. There is no divorce of his Bride.[47] There is instead the *sharing* of the kingdom / throne.

Perfectly consistent with all of this is:

➜ Revelation 22:1-3:
> "And he showed me a pure river of water of life, clear as crystal, proceeding from the throne of God and of the Lamb. In the middle of its street, and on either side of the river, was the tree of life, which bore twelve fruits, each tree yielding its fruit every

---

[46] Greg Beale, *New International Greek Testament Commentary, Revelation*, (Carlisle, Paternoster, 1999)929.

[47] We will have a good bit to say about the issue of the Wedding below. Suffice it to say for now that the idea of AD 70 being typological of the end of the Christian age demands a future divorcing of a harlot bride (the church) and the marrying of another Bride.

month. The leaves of the tree were for the healing of the nations. And there shall be no more curse, but the throne of God and of the Lamb shall be in it, and His servants shall serve Him."

So, we have a description of the post parousia New Creation. Has Christ abdicated? Hardly. Twice John writes of "the throne of the Father *and* the Lamb." There is undeniably no divorce, no abdication.

To be especially noted is that what is established in Revelation 11, which of course is recapitulated in chapters 21-22, is the "everlasting kingdom" i.e. the unending reign of Messiah. And, what we cannot miss is that the kingdom, where Messiah and the Father sit on the throne together is fully established at the destruction of the city "where the Lord was slain" (Revelation 11:8). This is the destruction of the city Babylon, full of the blood of the prophets, of Jesus, and Jesus' apostles and prophets.[48]

Now, if the New Jerusalem arrived in AD 70, at the fall of Jerusalem, and if the New Creation will stand forever, without end, then the idea that AD 70– the time of the Wedding and the end of the Old Covenant (the Old Marriage Covenant) was typological of the future cannot be right. That which has no end cannot end! That which came to its predicted end cannot foreshadow the end of that which inspiration says will never pass away.

There is much, much more that could be said in this regard, but space prevents. But, simply take a look at a few "bullet points."

✦ In Luke 1, the angel told Mary about the child she was to bear: "He will be great, and will be called the Son of the Highest; and the Lord God will give Him the throne of His father David. And He will reign

---

[48] See my *Who Is This Babylon?* for a full discussion of the identity of Babylon in Revelation. In sum, only one city fits the description of that harlot city, and that was Old Covenant Jerusalem. That book is available from Amazon, my websites and other retailers.

27

over the house of Jacob forever, and of His kingdom *there will be no end*" (Luke 1:32-35– *ouk estai telos*).

What the angel told Marry is contra the traditional views of what happens with Christ and the kingdom at the "end." Messiah would be given the throne of David– thus, the Davidic kingdom. And, of that kingdom, thus, *of his rule over that kingdom*, there would be no end. You cannot divorce Messiah's throne from his kingdom rule, and his rule on that throne would be *without end.*

✦ The Old Covenant world was predicted to "vanish away" and to be removed (Hebrews 8:13). Jesus said "heaven and earth shall pass, but my word will never pass away" (Matthew 24:35).

✦ Ephesians 3:20-21 says that there is to be glory in the church– this is the body of Christ established among men, for the ages to the ages. This is the term that Beale says means endlessness. So, it is the unending duty of the church, established among men, to give glory to God through service and proclamation of Christ and his gospel.

✦ Hebrews 12:21-28– The Old Covenant creation was being shaken, and that means it was being removed. That covenant world was no longer going to function in the manner that it was ordained and delivered. When it no longer would function in its divinely ordained manner, that signaled its removal.

In stark contrast, the writer says that the New Covenant kingdom being delivered to them at that time "cannot be removed" echoing Daniel 2:44; 7:13f.

The traditional futurist views of the end say that after the end, there will be no evangelism. There will be no on-going benevolent work of the church. The church will no longer be a teaching body, continually instructing its members in the deeper things of Christ. In other words, *the church will cease to function as divinely ordained and established!*

But, if the church ceases to function as it was divinely established to do, then it will, just like the Mosaic Covenant, pass away. But, both the OT and New say this cannot be.

Those who claim AD 70 was a type of the end of the Christian age are affirming the very thing the Bible says cannot and will not happen. They claim that end of the Old Covenant kingdom foreshadowed the end of the New Covenant kingdom. But, the Bible is clear, the New Covenant kingdom will never pass away. This means AD 70 was not a foreshadowing of the end of the (endless) Christian age.

---

The Bible clearly, undeniably, repeatedly says that the reign of Christ on the throne, his kingdom, *will never end.* His New Covenant can never cease to function as divinely ordained.

To suggest therefore that the end of the Old Covenant age foreshadows the end of the New Covenant age is a direct violation of these clear, undeniable and repeated statements of scripture.

**There is something fundamentally wrong with a doctrine that is willing to affirm the exact opposite of what the Bible teaches!**

---

## Reason #3 - Types Are Always *Inferior*– Anticipating Something *Better*

In my aforementioned debate with Joel McDurmon he affirmed that the physical things of the Old Covenant foreshadowed the spiritual realities of Christ. For instance, all of the Zion prophecies of the Old Testament "have been spiritualized and fulfilled in Christ." However, when pressed with the reality that this demands that the end of the millennium resurrection– posited by Isaiah 25 as occurring on Zion– has been fulfilled, McDurmon took the position that spiritual Zion foreshadows a literal, physical reality in the literal physical land.[49] So, McDurmon's hermeneutic is physical foreshadows spiritual, which then typifies physical.

This is really quite stunning I challenged McDurmon to document it from history, the patristics, the creeds, and most importantly scripture, but he did not even try.

The scriptures are clear that types always pointed to something better, and, this is critical, to things spiritual.

---

[49] McDurmon seemed not to grasp that his hermeneutic falsified his own objections to the dispensational theology of a restored, physical kingdom. In his writings against millennialism he emphasizes the spiritual fulfillment of what Old Covenant Zion foreshadowed. However, in our debate, he insisted on a yet future physical fulfillment of the Abrahamic land promises. But, that kind of literalization demands a literal Zion, does it not? With his hermeneutic then, McDurmon clearly opened the door for the millennialist to refute his eschatology.

Colossians 2:16-17– "So let no one judge you in food or in drink, or regarding a festival or a new moon or Sabbaths, which are a shadow of things to come, but the substance is of Christ."

A couple of things should be noted here. First, Paul says it was the Old Covenant praxis that were shadows. In stark contrast, he says Christ is the substance, the *body*, the reality.

Mathison speaks the truth when he says, "Believers are not to be judged on these matters because all of these things are but 'shadows.' The reality, of 'substance' belongs to Christ.... It is a contrast between two ages, the former age of shadows and the present age of the substance of Christ."[50] While this sounds good, in reality, many Dominionists insist that Christ and his work is in fact another shadow.

The late Greg Bahnsen for instance, commenting on the Sabbath, said, "At the coming of Christ the Sabbath was *purged* of the legalistic accretions brought by the scribes and Pharisees (Luke 13:10-17; 14:1-6; Mark 3:1-6); the Sabbath had suffered corruption at the hands of the autonomous Pharisees just as numerous other moral precepts had (cf. Matthew 5:21-48). Moreover, the *ceremonial and sacrificial aspects* of the Older Testamental cycle of feast days ('new moon, Sabbath year, Jubilee, etc.) along with those cyclic observances of feast days, were 'put out of gear' by Christ's work of redemption. Hence, Colossians 2:16f looses us from the ceremonial elements of the Sabbath system (the passage seems to be referring specifically to feast *offerings*), and passages such as Romans 15:5f and Galatians 4:10 teach that we need

---

[50] Keith Mathison, *From Age to Age: The Unfolding of Biblical Eschatology*, (Philippsburg, NJ, P & R Publishing, 2009)591. Of course, Mathison is just another example of Dominionists who say this, but then turn around and affirm that the events of AD 70 were typological of something yet to come.

not distinguish these ceremonial days any longer (as the Judaizers were apt to require.)." (P. 226-227– all emphasis his). The Sabbath was a shadow of coming salvation under Torah– Sabbath is now a shadow of coming salvation now. As Christ provides for entrance into eternal Sabbath rest of God by His substitutionary death upon the cross, He makes the typological elements (e.g. the offerings) of the Sabbath system irrelevant (things which were a shadow of the coming substance according to Colossians 2:157; Hebrews 10:1,8). By accomplishing our redemption Christ also binds us to the observance of that weekly Sabbath which prefigures our eternal Sabbath (cf. Hebrews 4)."[51]

So there you have it. The Old Covenant Sabbath foreshadowed the work of Christ *which now foreshadows things yet to come*. The trouble is, this flies directly in the face of what Colossians says. Where would one get from Colossians the idea that Christ and the New Covenant has become another system of types and shadows? It simply is not there.

**Hebrews 9:23f** – "Therefore it was necessary that the copies of the things in the heavens should be purified with these, but the heavenly things themselves with better sacrifices than these. For Christ has not entered the holy places made with hands, which are copies of the true, but into heaven itself, now to appear in the presence of God for us"

The Hebrews writer is clear that the earthly, Old Covenant temple and praxis was the shadow of the heavenly, spiritual, true and *better* realities. Christ became the minister of the True Tabernacle, the one not made with hands (Hebrews 8:1). But now, in the Dominionist hermeneutic, we have every right to ask if the spiritual temple of Christ foreshadows another, even better, even more spiritual– but decidedly *physical*-- temple. But, this raises a critical issue.

---

[51] Greg Bahnsen, *Theonomy in Christian Ethics*, (Nagadoches, Tx., Covenant Media Press, 2002)227.

The Old Covenant types pointed to something *better*. And, those types were supposed to pass / cease when the "better things" that they foreshadowed came to reality. In other words, the shadows would pass away because they were not effacious, *they were weak and ineffective. They were intended to be temporary* (cf. Hebrews 10:1-4).

We are now being told that the events of AD 70 foreshadowed future realities, i.e. the end of the Christian system. But, we must ask, why must the Christian age, the Christian system come to an end? *Why?*

James Jordan offered his take on this question in his "The Garden of God" tape series, "Each time God establishes a new heavens and earth there comes a time when that system he has set up runs its course, and is no longer operating (either due to sin or due to its historical inadequacy), then we see that the heavens and earth begin to break apart, and then be re-structured."[52] In his on line version of that work, he reiterates this principle: "At each stage of Biblical history, God lays hold of an existing deteriorating situation, breaks His people down through a death-resurrection transition, and reestablishes them with a renewed covenant. Each time God does this, He brings in a new covenant, a new stage of history, a new *world model."[53]*

This is quite good on many levels, but, it simply *does not apply to the Christian age*– the work of Christ. In fact, to suggest that the Christian age must come to an end strongly implies, if it does not actually demand, that there is something deeply, fundamentally wrong with the work of Christ.

---

[52] James Jordan, "The Garden of God," (1988) Tape 3, P. 1, my emp). I had a formal debate with Jordan in 2003, and I challenged him to demonstrate the weakness or insufficiency of the Christian age, since, per his hermeneutic, all ages must end because of deficiencies. He never offered a response. Audios of that debate are available from my websites. Also, a book of the debate is also available from me.

[53] http://www.biblicalhorizons.com/pdf/jjne.pdf

After all, we are told that all previous "worlds" came to an end in the various Days of the Lord. There were many ends of "heavens and earths" in the Old Covenant, *all because of the deficiencies and failures of those systems.* Their "deteriorating situation" demanded their end and the establishment of something *better.* "Due to sin or due to its historical inadequacy" all previous covenants and "worlds" came to an end. And all of this supposedly demands the ultimate end of the Christian age.

But again, *why did those kingdoms come to an end?*
They ended because they were *deficient.*
They ended because *they filled the measure of their sin.*
They ended because they were *man-made– made with hands.*
They ended because *they were not God's kingdom goal.*
They ended because God's eschatological promises were not fulfilled.

The great question is: Does any of this apply to the blood bought body of Christ?
Exactly how is the New Covenant of Christ deficient?
Will the body of Christ one day fill up the measure of sin?
Is the blood bought body of Christ a temple "made with hands"?
Is the church not the glorious expression of the kingdom of God?
What is the "sin and historical inadequacy" of the body of Christ?
Were the eschatological promises not being fulfilled in the first century, in the New Creation of Christ?

It seems more than apparent that not one of the reasons Jordan gives for the ending of all previous "old creations" applies to the church. So, if none of the reasons apply to the church and the current age, there is no reason for the church and the current age to come to an end.

Consider this: It seems to me if one if one accepts Jordan's arguments as valid, it negates the postmillennnial eschatology. After all, we are told the church and the church's righteous influence in the world will only continue to get better and better and stronger and stronger. But, if Jordan is right, and all ages / worlds come to an end due to their inadequacy, sin, and deficiency, then clearly, the Postmillennial view is false.

34

So, if the previous ages and systems ended because of inherent deficiencies and failures, we must press the question: What is wrong with the blood bought body of Christ, the Christian system, that demands that it must one day give way to....what?

So, according to scripture, types and shadows are always inferior. They always pointed to something better, something greater.[54] No where in scripture does it indicate the church is deficient, looking forward to something more "real", more "better." This negates the idea that AD 70 was a type of a yet future end of the Christian age.

**Some Dominionists insist that because all earlier systems came to an end– due to their inherent deficiencies and their sin– this somehow demands the end of the Christian age.**
**But, if this principle is true, in what way is the body of Christ ineffective, inefficient, inherently flawed and *sinful* to such an extent that it must come to an end?**

---

[54] It can also be argued that shadows always pointed to spiritual realities, not other physical things.

35

> **Reason #4 - No New Testament writer ever stated that the events of their day were typological of greater events to come.**

As we noted above, no Old Testament prophet ever hinted that the events of AD 70 were to be typological of greater events beyond that event. Like the OT prophets they cited, they predicted one eschatological consummation.

Let me reiterate: *No New Testament author ever stated that the events of AD 70 were typological.* This is significant. Hays, commenting on 1 Corinthians 10:6f says: "The events narrated in Scripture 'happened as *tupoi emon*' (10:6). The phrase does not mean—despite many translations—'warnings for us.' It means 'types of us,' prefigurations of the ekklesia. For Paul, Scripture, rightly read, prefigures the formation of the eschatological community of the church."[55] Do you catch that? "They were types of us," *not*, "We are types of something else."

While the New Testament writers positively affirm that the events that occurred in the Old Covenant days were types of what was happening in the days of the apostles, not one New Testament writer affirms that what was happening in their days was typological of what would happen at some distant point in the future. Not one of them *says,* "We are types of what is coming!" Nor do they say that what was happening in their day would happen over and over and again and again throughout history. As Goppelt says: "The NT's understanding and exposition of the OT lies at the heart of its theology, and it is primarily expressed within the framework of a typological

---

[55] Richard Hays, *Conversion of the Imagination* (Grand Rapids, MI: Eerdmans, 2005)11.

interpretation."[56] In stark contrast, no NT writer ever suggests that the NT is to be interpreted typologically of another age, another eschaton.

Concerning 1 Corinthians 10:6f, Barton notes, "Christians in Corinth are told, for example, that they are fortunate to be alive when the decisive moment in history came about. So the present has become the moment to which all the Scriptures have been pointing, though their meaning can only be understood with that divinely inspired intuition which flows from acceptance of the Messiah."[57] In other words, the goal of all previous ages had, in fact arrived—not a type or shadow of the "real" consummation or the true goal.[58]

As Wilkin notes, when the New Testament authors and early Christians thought of the events of their day, "Christians juxtaposed the 'types' of the OT and the 'truth' of the New. Earlier events were seen as figures or models that prefigured the spiritual events of the New. . . . the type was perishable, the spiritual reality eternal."[59]

So, the early church clearly did not see themselves as typological of anything. They believed that they were the *anti-types*– the fulfillment. Mbuvi says, "It is not merely that Christians are antitypes of Israel." He then cites Albert R. Jonsen who says, "They are, rather, rightfully

---

[56] Leonhard Goppelt, *Typos The Typological Interpretation of the Old Testament In The New*, (Grand Rapids, Eerdmans1982) (Foreword, XX).

[57] John Barton *The Biblical World*, Vol. 1 (New York: Routledge, 2004)142.

[58] See my article on 1 Corinthians 10:11, "The End of the Age Has Come," at www.eschatology.org/index.php?option=com_content&task=view&id=66&Itemid=61

[59] Robert Wilkin, *The Land Called Holy* (London: Yale University Press, 1992)326.

assumed to bear the promises of Israel as the recipients of the eschatological expectations of Israel."[60]

As a direct corollary to our point that no New Testament writer ever compared the fall of Jerusalem with anything beyond it, there is something else. They always compared the impending consummation with events that were *past*.[61]

Jesus compared his AD 70 parousia with the days of Noah (Matthew 24:37f),[62] not with any event beyond AD 70.[63] Likewise, he compared the days of Lot with his coming AD 70 parousia, but not with any

---

[60] Andrew M. Mbuvi, *Temple, Exile and Identity in 1 Peter* (T and T Clark International, 2001)31, n. 117.

[61] This is even true in 2 Peter 3, where Peter compares, just like Jesus did, the days of Noah with the impending Day of the Lord. Now, Peter was writing on the very cusp of the fall of Jerusalem and the end of the Old Covenant age. That cataclysm was, we are told, the penultimate type of the climax of the cosmos. Yet, Peter (supposedly) ignores that impending end of the age. He says not a word about what was about to happen was a sign of what would ultimately happen. Instead, he compares what was about to happen with the Noahic flood! Why, if AD 70 was the greatest of events, did Peter ignore that event, and compare the coming Day of the Lord to the Flood?

[62] This has tremendous implications for the proper interpretation of 2 Peter 3. If Jesus compared the Flood with AD 70, and if Peter compares the Flood with the impending Day of the Lord, then we have good reason to believe that Peter was, just like his master, comparing AD 70 with the Flood.

[63] I am cognizant that many believe Matthew 24:37 is a discussion of a yet-future, final coming of Christ. However, in my *We Shall Meet Him In The Air, the Wedding of the King of kings,* I demonstrate that this is untenable.

event beyond AD 70 (Luke 17:28).[64] Since no New Testament author ever suggests, in any way, that what was happening or about to happen was typological of yet-future events, it is unjustified to create such a doctrine.

This is why McDurmon's arguments in our debate are so disingenuous.[65]He admitted at least twice that the resurrection of 1 Corinthians 15 and Revelation 20 had "a fulfillment" in AD 70, because the language demands an imminent application and fulfillment, but there is still the "final fulfillment." The question is, as I said repeatedly, *where is the textual support for such a doctrine?* This idea is a theological invention, contrived out of the necessity to maintain a futurist eschatology. It is based on the misguided definition of the death of Adam, as we noted in the beginning of this book.[66]

Consider finally that when Paul said the end of the age had come, this means he was saying the end of "this present evil age" (Galatians 1:4)

---

[64] The same comparisons can be found in Jude and 2 Peter as well. Both authors were anticipating the imminent "telos" and compared it with former days and events– not with anything in the distant future. Jude unequivocally states that the last days foretold by the apostles and prophets were present in his day.

[65] McDurmon is not alone in his view. James Jordan, Kenneth Gentry and others, while perhaps not expressing the idea that 1 Corinthians 15 / Revelation 20 "had a fulfillment in AD 70," their suggestion that AD 70 was typological is perfectly consonant with McDurmon's posit.

[66] As I noted repeatedly in the debate, the Biblical writers were concerned with "the death" and "the curse" of Adam, and the solution to that "the death." I pointed out that in Revelation 21-22, in the New Creation which, again, McDurmon says came in AD 70, there is no more "the death" and "no more curse no more." McDurmon could only say that we do not know for certain that "the death" in Revelation is the Adamic death and curse!

was falling on them. This in turn means "the age to come" was about to fully arrive.

Note what McDurmon says in his comments on Hebrews 8:13f (cited below also); "As he wrote, in his time, the Old was becoming obsolete and was ready to vanish away. It has not yet been completely wiped out, but was certainly in its dying moments. It died in AD 70, when the symbol and ceremonies of that Old System– the Temple and the sacrifices– were completely destroyed by the Roman armies. This was the definitive moment when "this age' of Jesus and Paul ended and completely gave way to their 'age to come.' This, of course, is exactly why Jesus tied 'the end of the age' to His prophecy of the destruction of the Temple." (2011, 47). DeMar agrees that "the age to come" arrived in AD 70: "The old covenant age came to an end and was made 'obsolete' because of the work of Christ. (Hebrews 8:13). This resulted in 'the age to come' (Matthew 12:32), which incorporated believing Jews and Gentiles into the blessings of the 'new covenant in (Jesus') blood' (Luke 22:20)."[67]

There is something deeply ironic here. Most Dominionists (Postmillennialists) appeal constantly to the creeds and church history as at least in some manner a validation of their theology.[68] In fact, it

---

[67] Gary DeMar, *End Times Fiction*, (Nashville, Thomas Nelson, 2001)74).

[68] Of course, what the Dominionists do not tell you, and don't want you to know, is that Postmillenialism is *explicitly condemned* in some creeds! The Second Helvetic Confession (A.D. 1566) says: "We further condemn Jewish dreams that there will be a golden age on earth before the Day of Judgement, and that the pious, having subdued all their godless enemies, will possess all the kingdoms of the earth. For evangelical truth in Matt. chs. 24 and 25, and Luke, ch. 18 and the apostolic teaching in II Thess., ch. 2, and II Tim., chs. 3 and 4, present something quite different (Chap. 11, in *"Reformed Confessions of the 16th Century*, ed. Arthur C. Cochrane, Westminster Press, 1966). My thanks to Mike Bennett for sending this information. See below for more on

is often claimed that the full preterist view cannot be true because it is not "creedal." Yet, when it comes to the "age to come" something strange is taking place.

McDurmon, Gentry, Jordan and others openly say "the age to come" arrived in AD 70.

**Fact**: They cannot find this doctrine in the creeds!

**Fact**: While they say the age to come arrived in AD 70, they nonetheless say the age to come will one day come to a "cataclysmic end." As far as the creeds are concerned, "the age to come" has no end!

Notice what the Nicene Creed says: "He shall come again, with glory, to judge the quick and the dead; Whose kingdom *shall have no end...* and I look for the resurrection of the dead: and the life of the world to come." (Cited by DeMar, 2001, 213, My emphasis).

Notice how Dominionists contradict the creeds in regard to key eschatological tenets:

They believe Christ came in AD 70– non-Creedal.

They believe he came in glory in AD 70– non-Creedal.

They believe he judged the living and the dead (Revelation 11:15f) in AD 70– non-Creedal.

They believe the end of the age arrived in AD 70- non-Creedal.

They believe the age to come arrived in AD 70– non-Creedal.

They believe Christ's marriage was in AD 70- Non-Creedal.

They believe resurrection "a resurrection at least" occurred in AD 70- Non-Creedal.

They believe the New Heaven and Earth arrived in AD 70- non-Creedal.

They believe the "age to come" will one day end– non-Creedal.

In light of these facts one has the right to say the partial preterist Dominionists are also "partial-Creedalists"! In fact, one could make

---

this issue.

an *even more extensive* list of tenets in which Dominionists are at direct odds against the creeds.

Indeed, it is more than remarkable, not to mention duplicitous, in light of all of these non-Creedal positions held by the Dominionists that they point the accusing finger at advocates of Covenant Eschatology for being non-Creedal?

What is even more remarkable is that within the Reformed community there is currently a strong attack being made against the Postmillennial Dominion eschatology for being "non-Creedal." Prominent Amillennial Reformed ministers are accusing Postmillennialists of "heresy." It is being said that Dominionists cannot even be considered Reformed. It is said they are in violation of the creeds.[69] Irony of ironies!

Of course, back to our point: Biblically, as we have seen, the age to come would have *no end*. Thus, Paul's emphatic declaration that the end of "this age" had arrived is a definitive refutation of the idea that AD 70 was typological of another yet future eschaton. The current Christian age has no end. Thus, the end of the Mosaic age cannot have been a foreshadowing of the end of the endless age.

---

[69] See for instance the devastating critique by Rev. Ron Cammenga at:
http://www.mountainretreatorg.net/eschatology/creedamil.html
See also Prof. David Engelsma's critique:
http://www.graceonlinelibrary.org/eschatology/amillennialsm/reformed-amillennialism-an-introduction-by-prof-david-j-engelsma/

---

**Reason #5 -** **Jesus said the events of AD 70 were the greatest that had ever been, or that ever would be (Matthew 24:21). So, how can the greatest events in history- past or future- foreshadow even greater events?**

---

It must be kept in mind that types *always* go from the lesser to the greater in significance. So to suggest that any of these things listed above were typological of some yet-future event, or typological of events to be repeated over and over, demands that the yet-future events *must be greater and more meaningful than what happened in the life, ministry, resurrection and AD 70 parousia of Christ.* To suggest that anything could be greater than these things is surely dangerous: it is, at heart, an anti-gospel claim. Now consider this:

> "For then there will be great tribulation, such as has not been since the beginning of the world until this time, no, nor ever shall be (Matthew 24:21)."

Jesus said the events of the end of the Old Covenant age would be the greatest that had ever occurred *or that ever would occur!*

I concur with Gentry,[70] DeMar[71] and others who say when Jesus described the events leading up to and including the fall of Jerusalem as the greatest events in history, he was not focused strictly on the

---

[70] Kenneth Gentry, *He Shall Have Dominion* (Tyler, TX: Institute for Christian Economics, 1992)347. "I would argue: first, the covenantal significance of the loss of the temple stands as the most dramatic redemptive-historical outcome of the Jewish War."

[71] Gary DeMar, *Last Days Madness*, Revised Edition (Atlanta: American Vision, 1994)102f.

number of people who died, but rather on *the covenantal significance of the event*. Jesus was saying the events of the first century, namely, the Great Tribulation and his parousia, were to be the greatest *covenant events* that had ever occurred or that would ever occur! *Do you catch the power of that?*

Consider this: The Old Covenant could not give life or righteousness (Galatians 3:20-21). Life under Torah was to be "dead men walking" (Romans 7:4-14). That Covenant, as glorious as it was, simply exacerbated man's futility– his sin and death (Romans 5:20-21). It truly was a ministration of death (2 Corinthians 3:4f).

The New Covenant, established through the shedding of Jesus' blood, provides everything that Torah could never give (Acts 13:39). It is the ministration of life and frees believers from the law of sin and death (Romans 8:1-3).

And yet, we are told this New Covenant ministry will one day be terminated, cease to function! No more grace extended. Time will end, human history will be over.

The question is, would not the termination of the New Covenant of grace be far, far greater than the end of the "ministration of death"? Would not the "end of time" and destruction of the material cosmos be exponentially far greater than the fall of Jerusalem– even on a purely physical basis?

In point of fact, everything about the futurism of today, would be so far "greater," bigger, more cataclysmic than the events of AD 70 that there could be no comparison, either on a covenantal level or on a physical level. All of which flies in the face of Jesus' words.

Riddlebarger says we must accept the AD 70 fulfillment of these words, and yet then argues for a "double fulfillment" (2003, 170). This is patently illogical, however. How can it be affirmed that the AD 70 event was the greatest event *that ever had occurred or would ever occur*, per Jesus, and then turn around and claim that the greatest event ever signified another, greatest (actually greater!) event ever?

Virtually all books on hermeneutics acknowledge that types always move from the lesser to the greater. Since the New Covenant of grace is greater than the Torah, would not the end of the gospel of grace be more catastrophic? Surely, as we just suggested, the end of the gospel, purchased by the Son of God's blood, would be greater than anything else that had or could occur. Would not *the end of time* be far greater than the fall of Jerusalem and the end of the Old Covenant theocracy?

I am confident everyone would agree that anything associated with the traditional views of eschatology—that is, the end of time, the destruction of the cosmos, the end of the Christian age, etc.—would be far greater in scope and meaning than the fall of Jerusalem and the end of the Old Covenant age. Yet, Jesus leaves no room for argumentation.

He said the events surrounding the end of that Old Covenant age would be the greatest ever. How then is it possible to argue that Christ's AD 70 parousia was simply typological? Logically, scripturally, textually, you cannot tenably make that argument. There can be nothing greater than the greatest event that had ever occurred *or that ever would occur.* Yet, this is what is demanded by the argument that AD 70 was a type of the end of the world. This is a contradiction of Jesus' statements.

A side bar here on the significance of the Olivet Discourse in eschatological studies. As Mathison says, "The interpretation of Jesus' Olivet Discourse will have a profound effect upon any study of eschatology."[72] When disputing with Dispensationalists,. Gentry likewise emphasizes the centrality of the Discourse. However, aware that a growing number of Postmillennialists are adopting a "united Discourse" view, Gentry has begun to equivocate, going so far as to say, if it could be proven that the Discourse were a united discussion of the AD 70 events, that it would not seriously impact his futurist eschatology. This is patently false, and fellow Reformed scholars

---

[72] Keith Mathison, *Postmillennialism: An Eschatology of Hope*, (Philippsburg, NJ, P&R Publishing, 1999)111.

45

know this. In fact, some Reformed Amillennialists say that to surrender any part of the Discourse to AD 70 is to surrender essential doctrinal truth.

In a strident condemnation of Gentry, DeMar, Mathison and other Postmillennialists, Reformed Amillennialist David Engelsma says: "Such is the basic importance of the prophecy of Matthew *on the reckoning of everyone* that if Jesus' eschatology has only the destruction of Jerusalem in view the same is true of all the eschatology of the New Testament. Matthew 24 is the issue. The interpretation of Matthew 24 is the difference between the hope of the Christian faith and the hopelessness of preterism."[73] (His emphasis).

I concur with Engelsma that the Discourse is foundational to an understanding of Biblical eschatology and that it is disingenuous to divorce it from the rest of the NT teaching. You cannot "surrender" Matthew 24:36-25:46 to an A. D. 70 application – as an increasing number of Dominionists do– without surrendering *all* futurist doctrines of judgment and resurrection. It is that simple.

This is illustrated in DeMar's *Last Days Madness* book in which he adduces numerous parallels between the Discourse and both 1 and 2 Thessalonians, and concludes: "There are striking parallels between the Olivet Discourse and 2 Thessalonians 2. The events described in Matthew 24 were fulfilled prior to Jerusalem's destruction in AD 70. We should expect the same for 2 Thessalonians 2."[74]

---

73

http://www.mountainretreatorg.net/eschatology/preterist.html.
Engelsma and other leading Reformed Amillennialists say Dominionism is condemned in the creeds. It is heretical and soul damning. My thanks to Michael Bennett for the link.

[74] Gary DeMar, *Last Days Madness: Obsession of the Modern Church*, (Powder Springs, GA, American Vision, 1994)325.

46

What DeMar conveniently fails to tell his readers is that while there are indeed "striking parallels" between the Discourse and 2 Thessalonians, there are equally "striking parallels" between 1 Thessalonians 4:13f and Matthew 24:29f! Gentry acknowledges these parallels, going so far as to say the Discourse is the source of 1 Thessalonians 4: "Most commentators agree that the Olivet Discourse 'is undoubtedly a source of the Thessalonian Epistles.'" (Citing D.A. Carson, with approval).[75] Weima says Paul is referring, "to an authoritative teaching of Jesus Christ."[76] Likewise, Beale says, "Paul is recollecting the words of the earthly Jesus and paraphrasing him. This is apparent from noticing that 4:15-5:7 has numerous parallels[77] that demonstrate a high probability that Paul is dependent on Jesus' teaching on the last things."

The perfect, direct, multiple parallels between Matthew 24:29-31 and 1 Thessalonians 4:13-18 are undeniable. So, if one grants, as most Amillennialists and Postmillennialists do, that Matthew 24:29f referred to AD 70, then how is it possible to maintain a futurist view

---

[75] Kenneth Gentry: *Thine is the Kingdom,* (Vallecito, CA, Calcedon, 2003)162.

[76] Jeffrey Wiema, in *Commentary on the New Testament Use of the Old Testament*, Greg Beale and D. A. Carson, editors, (Grand Rapids, Baker Academic, 2007)880.

[77] Beale gives a list of 13 parallels between the Olivet Discourse and 1 Thessalonians 4:13-5:7–which as will see momentarily, is a very short list of the parallels. Significantly, Beale conveniently omits the direct parallel in the time statements! Jesus emphatically said that all of the things listed would be fulfilled in his generation. Paul said, "we who are alive and remain until the coming of the Lord." Of course, Beale expends considerable effort to show that neither Jesus nor Paul really meant to express the imminence that their words would normally indicate. Greg Beale, *1-2 Thessalonians, The IVP New Testament Series,* (Downers Grove, ILL, InterVarsity Press, 2003)136.

of Thessalonians? In numerous formal written and public debates, I have yet to receive an answer to this challenge.

So, to return to our point. Jesus said the events of the end of the age parousia in AD 70 would be the greatest events ever– past or future. The futurists apply 1 Thessalonians 4 to the future, and describe it as an event that would make AD 70 pale in significance. This is a blatant contradiction of Jesus' words, and therefore false. This means that AD 70 was not typological of a yet future, greater event.

> **The end of time, the destruction of the universe, the termination of the gospel of grace, would be exponentially "greater", on virtually every level, than the events of AD 70.**
>
> **Jesus said the events surrounding the end of the Old Covenant age were the greatest that had ever been, or ever would be!**
>
> **It is therefore, patently wrong to say those greatest ever events somehow foreshadowed events that make the first century events pale in significance.**

**Reason #6 - Jesus Said The Events of AD 70 Would Be When "All Things That Are Written must Be Fulfilled" (Luke 21:22). This Means There Could Not Be Any Additional Eschatology Beyond AD 70.**

Very clearly, if Jesus meant to say that in the events of AD 70 all prophecy was to be fulfilled, then all futurist paradigms are falsified. The partial preterists feel the power of this and have attempted to respond.

Gentry feels he has definitively refuted the idea that Jesus was referring to all things written, comprehensively speaking, and thereby refuted the full preterist claims. What follows, in edited form, is my response to Gentry's claims.

Gentry takes every opportunity to condemn preterists, but he refuses to actually engage in honorable discussions *with* preterists. He has been challenged *many* times by *numerous* people, including myself, to meet me in formal public debate. He invariably refuses.

As noted, Gentry clearly thinks he has found a fatal flaw in the preterist argument on Luke 21:22. Here is Gentry's argument from an Internet article:[78]

<In its context Luke 21:22 reads as follows: "But when you see Jerusalem surrounded by armies, then recognize that her desolation is at hand. Then let those who are in Judea flee to the mountains and let those who are in the midst of the city depart and let not those who are

---

78

http://net.bible.org/verse.php?book=luk&chapter=21&verse=2 2>

in the country enter the city; because these are days of vengeance, in order that all things which are written may be fulfilled" (Lk 21:20-22).

Inarguably, (sic) the context here is focusing on AD 70, as even dispensationalists agree.

The hyper-preterists naively assume that Jesus is speaking globally of absolutely all prophecies when he declares that "all things which are written" will be fulfilled in AD 70. They hold, therefore, that no prophecy remains, which means that prophecies regarding the resurrection of all men, the second coming, and more came to pass in AD 70. They base their argument on deficient hermeneutics. Note just one deadly observation against their approach: The grammar of the passage limits the declaration. Jesus speaks of "all things which are written" by employing a perfect passive participle: /gegrammena /("having been written"). This refers to prophecies already written — when he speaks in AD 30. Yet we know that more prophecies arise later in the New Testament revelation.

Once again we see a limitation on Jesus' statement. Furthermore, technically it does not even refer to any prophecy which Christ speaks. For these are not prophecies that have already been written. That being the case, the final resurrection (for instance) is outside of this declaration (Jn 5:28-29).

Thus, Jesus is referring to all things written in the Old Testament. At this stage of redemptive history those are the only prophecies that had already been written. (EoQ, DKP)

Quite frankly, *I could hardly believe what I was reading* from the pen of the erudite Dr. Gentry. He has engaged in numerous debates. He surely knows one must be careful in making polemic arguments. The absolute desperation, the *total failure of logic* on the part of Dr. Gentry is glaring and egregious.

Let me summarize Dr. Gentry's argument for ease of understanding.

**When Jesus said (Luke 21:22), that "all things written must be fulfilled," he referred only to those prophecies (and *all* of those prophecies), that had been written prior to his statement in AD 30.**

**All New Testament prophecies of the resurrection (e.g. John 5:28f, 1 Corinthians 15, 1 Thessalonians, etc.), were written after AD 30.**

**Therefore, all New Testament prophecies of the resurrection were not part of the "all things that are written" that were to be fulfilled in the fall of Jerusalem in AD 70.**

Here is what Dr. Gentry concludes: "Thus, Jesus is referring to all things written in the Old Testament. At this stage of redemptive history those are the only prophecies that had already been written."

Gentry's "logic," if such it can be called, fails on a number of points. However, I will only make two points in response to Dr. Gentry's amazing argument.

**Argument #1**– The New Testament prophecies of the resurrection are simply the reiteration of the Old Testament prophecies *(things already written in A.D. 30)*.
**Proof of this argument**: I need only refer to the words of Paul. The apostle affirmed in the most unambiguous manner that his doctrine of the resurrection was *nothing* but what was found in the Old Testament, i.e. *in that which had already been written*!

**Acts 24:14-15:** "But this I confess to you, that according to the Way which they call a sect, so I worship the God of my fathers, believing all things which are written in the Law and in the Prophets. I have hope in God, which they themselves also accept, that there will be a resurrection of the dead, both of the just and the unjust."
Paul said his doctrine of the resurrection of the dead, for which he was on trial, was found in Moses and the Law and the prophets. That certainly qualifies as that which was written before A.D. 30.

**Acts 26:21-23–** "Having therefore obtained help of God, I continue unto this day, witnessing both to small and great, saying none other things than those which the prophets and Moses did say should come: That Christ should suffer, and that he should be the first that should rise from the dead, and should shew light unto the people, and to the Gentiles."

Paul said he preached nothing, *nothing* but the hope of Israel found in Moses and the prophets. *Do you catch the power of that?*
**Paul taught of the resurrection of the dead.**

**But, Paul did not preach anything but the hope of Israel found in Moses and the prophets.**

**Therefore, the doctrine of the resurrection of the dead was found in Moses and the prophets.**

**Romans 8:23– 9:1-4--** "And not only they, but ourselves also, which have the first fruits of the Spirit, even we ourselves groan within ourselves, waiting for the *adoption*, to wit, the redemption of our body... For I could wish that myself were accursed from Christ for my brethren, my kinsmen according to the flesh: 4 Who are Israelites; *to whom pertaineth the adoption*, and the glory, and the covenants, and the giving of the law, and the service of God, and the promises."
The adoption, according to Paul, was the resurrection.
But, the promise of the adoption was given to, and belonged to, Israel after the flesh.
This means the adoption, the promise of the resurrection, was from the Old Testament prophecies.

**1 Corinthians 15:54-55--** "So when this corruptible shall have put on incorruption, and this mortal shall have put on immortality, then shall be brought to pass the saying that is written, Death is swallowed up in victory. O death, where is thy sting? O grave, where is thy victory?"
Paul cites Isaiah 25:8 and Hosea 13:14 as the source of his resurrection doctrine in Corinthians.

Paul said the resurrection would be when Isaiah 25 and Hosea 13:14 would be fulfilled.

Thus, the resurrection hope and doctrine of 1 Corinthians 15 was found in, and based on the Old Testament prophecies made to Israel.

From these texts, it is undeniable that the resurrection hope expressed by the New Testament writers was nothing other than a reiteration of what had already been written long ago in the Old Testament scriptures! This is *fatal* to Gentry's argument and theology.

It is simply wrong to say the New Testament prophecies of the resurrection are not grounded in and based on the Old Covenant prophecies. This is to deny Paul who said he preached nothing but the hope of Israel found in Moses and the prophets. 1 Corinthians 15 is not different from Isaiah 25 or Hosea 13:14, for Paul says that when the resurrection occurred, it would be the fulfillment of those prophecies. To say 1 Corinthians 15 is the explication of those prophecies is not the same as saying they are different from those prophecies.

Therefore, you cannot say all Old Testament prophecies were fulfilled at the AD 70 parousia of Christ,, without affirming the fulfillment of all New Testament eschatology. There is no "new" eschatology in the New Testament. *All New Testament eschatology is the anticipation of the imminent fulfillment of Old Testament promises.* Period. This totally falsifies Gentry's specious argument.

It is interesting, to say the least, to witness Gentry's on-going "conversion" in regard to resurrection and the Old Covenant prophecies. For instance, Gentry has historically applied Daniel 12:2 to the "end of the world."[79] However, he now says, "Daniel appears to be presenting Israel as a grave site under God's curse; Israel as a

---

[79] Kenneth Gentry, *The Greatness of the Great Commission*, (Tyler, Tx., Institute for Christian Economics, 1993)142.

corporate body is in the dust (Daniel 12:2; cp. Ge. 3:14, 19). In this he follows Ezekiel's pattern in his vision of the dry bones, which represents Israel's 'death' in the Babylonian dispersion (Ezekiel 37). In Daniel's prophecy many will awaken, as it were, during the great tribulation to suffer the full fury of divine wrath, while others will enjoy God's grace in receiving everlasting life" (*Dominion*, 2009, 538).

So, Gentry now applies Daniel 12 to AD 70. This is, needless to say, a *radical* change from his earlier view, yet he has given no indication noting that change.[80] This likewise puts him at odds with the huge majority of scholarship, church history and the creeds. One can but wonder if the on-going controversy with what Gentry disparagingly calls "hyper-preterism" has spawned Gentry's "conversion."

So, consider what this does for Dr. Gentry:

**All Old Testament prophecy would be fulfilled by the time of, and in the events of the fall of Jerusalem in AD 70. (Gentry)**

**But, the Old Testament predicted the general resurrection of the dead (Paul– Acts 24; 26; 1 Corinthians 15)**

---

[80] Interestingly, in his 2009 *Dominion*, (495, n. 45) Gentry takes note that Dispensationalist Dwight Pentecost had radically altered his views over the years yet had not acknowledged or indicated that change in his later writings. He says Pentecost's "radical shift" in his application of some key eschatological texts, "does not seem to him to compromise his eschatological system." Gentry has made an astoundingly radical shift in his application of one of the key eschatological texts, yet has not indicated that change in his writings so far as we can determine. He has *done* what he chides Pentecost for doing!

**Therefore, the general resurrection of the dead occurred in the events of the fall of Jerusalem in AD 70.**

We have established point #1 beyond any possibility of refutation. This point alone totally destroys Gentry's attempt at refuting Covenant Eschatology.

**Argument #2**– For argument sake therefore, I will most gladly accept Dr. Gentry's own summary statement: "Thus, Jesus is referring to *all things written in the Old Testament*. At this stage of redemptive history those are the only prophecies that had already been written." (My emphasis, DKP)

Consider then the following argument:

**All things written in the Old Testament, i.e. all Old Testament prophecy, was fulfilled by the time of, and in the events of, the fall of Jerusalem in AD 70. (Gentry).**

**But, the Old Testament prophesied of the resurrection of the dead (Acts 24:14f; 26:6f; 26:21f, Romans 8:23-9:1-4, 1 Corinthians 15:55-56).**

**Therefore, the prophecies of the resurrection of the dead were fulfilled by the time of, and in the events of, the fall of Jerusalem in AD 70.**

This argument is *prima facie* true.

It is *incontrovertibly true* that the Old Testament foretold the resurrection of the dead. Gentry agrees.

It is *irrefutably true* that all New Testament prophecies of the resurrection are drawn from and the reiteration of the Old Testament prophecies.

It is *undeniable* that Jesus said all things written would be fulfilled by the time of, and in the events of the fall of Jerusalem in A.D. 70.

Gentry is correct in affirming that *all Old Testament prophecies* would be fulfilled at / in AD 70. And this proves, *beyond refutation*, that the resurrection of the dead came at the dissolution of the Old Covenant age of Israel in AD 70.[81]

Incidentally, it would do no good for Gentry, or anyone else, to amend his statement and argue that all Jesus really meant was that all Old Covenant prophecies *concerning the fall of Jerusalem* were to be fulfilled in AD 70. (Note Gentry made no attempt to limit the scope of the Old Covenant prophecies to be fulfilled in AD 70. He said emphatically, "Jesus is referring to *all things written in the Old Testament*").

The indisputable fact is that in the Old Testament the resurrection of the dead is *repeatedly* posited at the destruction of Old Covenant Israel. Note a couple of examples.

> Isaiah 25:1-8– "O LORD, You are my God. I will exalt You, I will praise Your name, For You have done wonderful things; Your counsels of old are

---

[81] See my presentation on "The Preterist Perspective of the Millennium." I presented this paper at Criswell College in October of 2012, demonstrating how the OT not only foretold the end of the millennium resurrection, but, emphatically and repeatedly posited it at the time of the avenging of the blood of the martyrs. Jesus' teaching in Matthew 23 definitively posits that as AD 70. Also, in my formal debate with McDurmon, my main point was proving that the OT posited the end of the millennium resurrection at the end of Israel's covenant age. The Criswell CD is available free of charge from me– just pay postage. DVDs of the McDurmon debate are available from my websites. The book form of that debate should be available shortly.

faithfulness and truth. 2 For You have made a city a ruin, A fortified city a ruin, A palace of foreigners to be a city no more; It will never be rebuilt. Therefore the strong people will glorify You; The city of the terrible nations will fear You. For You have been a strength to the poor, A strength to the needy in his distress, A refuge from the storm, A shade from the heat; For the blast of the terrible ones is as a storm against the wall. You will reduce the noise of aliens, As heat in a dry place; As heat in the shadow of a cloud, The song of the terrible ones will be diminished. And in this mountain The LORD of hosts will make for all people A feast of choice pieces, A feast of wines on the lees, Of fat things full of marrow, Of well–refined wines on the lees. And He will destroy on this mountain The surface of the covering cast over all people, And the veil that is spread over all nations. He will swallow up death forever, And the Lord GOD will wipe away tears from all faces; The rebuke of His people He will take away from all the earth; For the LORD has spoken."

Note that in the day that YHVH would destroy death, it would also be when He made the city a desolation and turned the temple over to foreigners. The city under consideration is the "city of confusion" in chapter 24:10f, Ariel, i.e. Jerusalem. So, Isaiah emphatically posits the resurrection at the time of Jerusalem's demise.

In chapter 26:19-21, the Lord predicted the resurrection at the time when YHVH would come out of heaven and avenge the blood of the martyrs. Of course, Jesus was emphatically clear that all of the righteous blood of all the saints, shed on the earth, would be avenged in the judgment of Jerusalem in A.D. 70 (Matthew 23:34f).

In Isaiah 27:1f, we find the destruction of Leviathan, the enemy of God, defeated in the day of the Lord's coming. This is the Day of

26:19f, i.e. the day of the resurrection. And, this Day of the Lord would also be when the people YHVH had created would no longer receive mercy. He would turn the altar to chalk stones (Isaiah 27:9f). Thus, again, the resurrection is clearly placed in the context of the judgment of Jerusalem and Israel.

There are in fact several OT passages which posit the resurrection in the context of the judgment of Israel. It is of interest to me that other than Daniel 12 on which he has changed his views, I have found little comment from Gentry about the OT predictions of the resurrection. In his massive tome of 2009, he does not mention Isaiah 25-27 or Hosea,[82] even though Paul cited these verses as the source of his resurrection doctrine in 1 Corinthians 15:54f.

The point of course is that it will do Gentry no good whatsoever to now say that all Jesus really meant to say was "these be the days of vengeance in which all things that are written about the fall of Jerusalem will be fulfilled." On one level, we could agree with this, for as it has been demonstrated, the fall of Jerusalem was in fact to be the time of the resurrection.

Gentry has, *through his own argument*, destroyed his Postmillennial, futurist eschatology. He has actually confirmed the truthfulness of "hyper-preterism!" And along the way, he has falsified the claim that the events of AD 70 were typological of another resurrection. If all OT prophecies have been fulfilled, then since the OT predicted the final, end of the millennium resurrection, clearly, the fulfillment of those eschatological prophecies was not typological of anything else in our future.

---

[82] Interestingly, Gentry does comment on Isaiah 26 as the final resurrection in his 1992 version of *Dominion* (p. 283, 284).

**Reason #7– The Restoration of All Things Would Be Consummated at the Parousia– Which Would Be At the End of the Old Covenant Age of Israel**

"Repent therefore and be converted, that your sins may be blotted out, so that times of refreshing may come from the presence of the Lord, and that He may send Jesus Christ, who was preached to you before, whom heaven must receive until the times of restoration of all things, which God has spoken by the mouth of all His holy prophets since the world began. For Moses truly said to the fathers, 'The Lord your God will raise up for you a Prophet like me from your brethren. Him you shall hear in all things, whatever He says to you. And it shall be that every soul who will not hear that Prophet shall be utterly destroyed from among the people.' Yes, and all the prophets, from Samuel and those who follow, as many as have spoken, have also foretold these days" (Acts 3:19-24).

V irtually all futurist eschatologies posit Acts 3:19-24 as a prediction of the "end of time," the time of the Second Coming of Christ at the end of the Christian age. This is true especially of the Amillennial and Postmillennial constructs.[83] What is particularly significant is the Dominionists all seem to agree the work of the "restoration of all things" began in the first century.

---

[83] It is interesting to say the least to see the contortions of many Postmillennialists when it comes to Acts 3. It is becoming increasingly common to read that Acts 3 definitely has an AD 70 application, but of course, it is then claimed, again, that AD 70 was only typological. However, the point is that more and more, postmillennialists agree there was an imminent fulfillment– at least in some way– of Acts 3. This is almost unprecedented in Reformed history.

Gentry, commenting on Acts 3 says: "This 'restoration of all things' begins in the first century during the ministry of Christ. John Calvin notes in this regard that 'Christ by His death has already restored all things...but the effect of it is not yet fully seen, because the restoration is still in process of completion, and so too our redemption.' In fact, Peter informs his auditors of the events begun in their time: 'Yes, and all the prophets, from Samuel and those who follow, as many as have spoken, have also foretold these days (Acts 3:24). This contemporary focus is also clear from Matthew 17:11, where John Baptist functions as an Elijah introducing the restoration of all things in the New Covenant (cf. Malachi 4:5-6)" (2009, 501).

He continues with his discussion of how the heavens must receive Christ until the restoration: "The force of the 'until' (until the times of restoration, DKP) makes the times of restitution simultaneous with Christ's mediatorial session in heaven. He will come again not to introduce the restitution predicted by the prophets, but because He shall then have completed it." (Ibid)

Mathison agrees with Gentry. Commenting on Matthew 9:18-34 and the healing of the blind. He says this is the fulfillment of Isaiah 35:5-6 and then says, "His healing of the blind and the mute indicates that the prophesied time of the eschatological restoration has arrived (Isaiah 35:5-6) (*Age*, 2009, 357).

The admission that the restoration of all things had begun and was to be perfected at the parousia is, in fact, a fatal admission for the Dominionists. Keep in mind the postmillennialists freely admit Christ came, the kingdom came in power and glory, the (a) resurrection and the judgment all occurred in AD 70. See the documentation later in this work. So, the question becomes, if the work of the restoration of all things *began with John* in the first century, and if all of the NT writers spoke of the imminent consummation, where is the justification for extrapolating that end into a far distant future?

This question is particularly important in light of the fact Peter said all of the Old Covenant prophets foretold the restoration of all things. And, this is where it is troublesome for the claim that AD 70 was typological of the real restoration of all things, Peter said all of those prophets "spoke of (his) these days" (Acts 3:24). Keep in mind Gentry's claim that all OT prophecy would be fulfilled in the events of AD 70. As we noted, this is a fatal admission.

Peter's affirmation that the OT prophets foretold his day is repeated by the apostle in 1 Peter 1:10-12 where he discusses the impending parousia of Christ to bring salvation (which is, of course, the time of the restoration of all things, the time when man could enter the Most Holy Place, etc.).

Notice Peter said the OT prophets were told the last days parousia for salvation was not for their day. However, through the Spirit, the time and manner of that eschatological climax was being revealed and fulfilled in Peter's day. In unmistakable terms, the apostle said Christ was "ready to judge the living and the dead" (1 Peter 4:5). The end of all things has drawn near" (4:7), and, "the time has come for the judgment to begin" (4:17).

So, the time of salvation foretold by the OT prophets was now, in unmistakable, unequivocal, emphatic words, declared to be imminent. This means Peter's comments that those OT prophets "spoke of these days" cannot mean Peter was saying those prophets spoke of days in the far distant future. He said they spoke of the consummation that, when he wrote 1 Peter, had drawn near.

Remember, in Acts 2:15f Peter emphatically said the Old Testament prophets foretold the last days– the time appointed for the restoration of all things. The fisherman cited the prophecy of Joel 2:28f and declared in no uncertain terms "this is that which was spoken by the prophet Joel." So, in both Acts 2 and Acts 3 the apostle undeniably tells us the prophesied time, the time for the restoration of all things, was present in the first century. What they were waiting on was the completion, the time when Christ would finish putting down his enemies at his parousia.

Note in Acts 2 Peter not only said the OT prophecies were being fulfilled, he urged them to beware of refusing the invitation to redemption and salvation. He also told them "save yourselves from this untoward generation" (Acts 2:40). This too drives home the contemporary nature of Peter's statement that the prophets foretold "these days." Peter was not looking far down the stream of time to a judgment at a distant Day of the Lord. He was anticipating some cataclysmic event in his generation. He was alluding to the Great and Terrible Day of the Lord that John, as Elijah, had proclaimed.

Space forbids a full discussion of John as Elijah.[84] However, Jesus emphatically declared John to be Elijah and he came "to restore all things" (Matthew 17:10f). Jesus used the verbal form of *apokatastasis*, the word translated as restoration in Acts 3.

So, John was Elijah. Elijah was to come "before the Great and Terrible Day of the Lord"[85] which is nothing less than the restoration

---

[84] I am currently working on a book on this very topic. The eschatological significance of John, as Elijah, is, in my estimation, one of the most overlooked topics in the entire study of eschatology. We find echoes of his message throughout the NT, yet, while some commentators will acknowledge this, they seem oblivious to the implications.

[85] It is critical to note that the Day of the Lord which John as Elijah was to proclaim was the Lord's coming in application of Mosaic Covenant Wrath, per Malachi 3:1-6. Elijah, thus John's, message to Israel was to observe the Law of Moses (Malachi 4:5) and violation of Torah would bring about the application of the Law of Blessings and Cursings. This means the Day of the Lord would be related, not to the Christian age, but to the Mosaic age and was to be a time of national judgment. See my book *From Torah To Telos: The*

of all things.[86] If John as Elijah was doing the work of the restoration of all things– and Jesus said he was– and if Peter was predicting the restoration of all things, then notice what we have.

John said the kingdom (the restoration of all things) "has drawn near." He said the precursory Tribulation i.e. the "wrath about to come" (from *mello*, meaning about to) was near.

As Hagner says (on Matthew 17), "John serves as a transition to the new (order, dkp)." "What has been implied through the quotation of Malachi 3:1 in v. 10 now comes to exact expression: *autos estin elias ho mellown erchetai*: 'he himself is Elijah' the one about to come.' What is meant here is not that he is Elijah *redivivus* (which is possibly what John denies according to John 1:21) but that he functions in the role that was ascribed to Elijah just preceding the end time... The expectation of the coming of Elijah prior to the end is found in Sirach 48:10."[87]

Davies and Allison, commenting on Matthew 3:7 also note the imminence in John's message: "'Who has warned you to flee from the

---

*End of the Law of Moses,* available from my websites, and other retailers. Also on Kindle.

[86] As I document in the book on John / Elijah, the prophet was to come before the Tribulation and the resurrection. So, if the resurrection is tied to Elijah and if John was Elijah, then John's declaration that the Day of the Lord (the kingdom) was near is nothing less than a declaration of the imminent resurrection. Thus, the consummation of the "restoration of all things" was to occur in John's generation.

[87] Donald Hagner, *Word Biblical Commentary, Matthew, Vol. 33,* (Dallas, Word, 1993)308. See also, James Dunn, *Word Biblical Commentary*, Vol. 38, 468)– on Romans 8:18– "It is natural to hear in the *mello* the note not only of certainty (see 8:13) but of imminence."

wrath about to come',... "*mello* here implies not so much purpose as imminence or futurity."[88]

Even Gentry acknowledges John's role as Elijah and that he initiated the consummative restoration of all things: "The evidence is really quite clear that Malachi's Elijianic prophecy was fulfilled during the ministry of Christ. This fulfillment is counter-indicative to both dispensationalism's hermeneutic and its eschatology, as well as being supportive of the preteristic hermeneutic and Postmillennial eschatology" (1992,367).

While Gentry claims the appearance of John as Elijah is "counter-indicative" to Dispensationalism, I suggest that his admissions concerning John and the restoration *are fatal to his Postmillennialism.* John did for certain initiate the restoration of all things. Jesus established this. But, John likewise said the consummation– the Great Day of the Lord– was near. Thus, the completion of the work initiated, the consummation of the restoration of all things, had drawn near. Gentry, as all futurists, simply ignores the inseparable connection between John's initiatory work and the imminent climax he preached.

The axe was already at the root, an echo of Malachi 4:1f, and "the winnowing fork is already in his hand." John spoke of the harvest– resurrection imagery-- and the burning up of the chaff. These images are not only eschatological motifs but communicate an undeniable imminence.

This demands that the restoration of all things which Peter ties to the coming of Christ would be the finalization of John's work. So, note the following:

John was Elijah, per Jesus.

---

[88] W. D. Davies and Dale Allison, *International Critical Commentary, Matthew 1-7,* (London, T and T Clark)304.

He initiated the "restoration of all things."

The restoration was to be completed at the Great Day of the Lord. Therefore, since John proclaimed the imminence of the Day of the Lord, it is *prima facie* true that the completion of the restoration of all things was truly, objectively near in the first century. This means the judgment John proclaimed was not, and could not be, a type or foreshadowing of another restoration of all things. John did not predict a near Day of the Lord and a far Day of the Lord.

Now, if the Dominionists insist on the multiple fulfillment of prophecy and that the first century events foreshadowed the future end times, then there is every reason to believe there is another Elijah, another John the Baptizer, yet to come. But this cannot be.

Remember, Jesus said John was the predicted Elijah and he came to restore all things. Likewise, Peter said the OT prophecies of the restoration of all things spoke of his first century generation "these days." In other words, the OT prophets, as we have seen above, foretold one eschatological consummation.

John did not come as Elijah, to predict the coming of another Elijah. He did not come to initiate a restoration typological of the real restoration of all things. There is simply no justification for suggesting John as Elijah was a foreshadowing of yet future far distant events. The *telos*, the end, he predicted was near.

I know of no Postmillennialist who affirms that John was typological of another Elijah. Yet, it surely seems to be demanded by their hermeneutic. After all, if the first Elijah was typological of the second Elijah (I.e. the Baptizer) then why wasn't John typological of the "real, literal, physical" Elijah who must yet come?

Do we not, based on the Dominionist hermeneutic of multiple fulfillments of prophecy, have every right to expect the coming of the real, physical, literal Elijah? Remember that McDurmon, in our debate, said the physical types foreshadowed the spiritual realities which in turn point to physical realities.

So, again, if the first Elijah was typological of the second Elijah (John) then why wasn't John typological of the "real, literal, physical" Elijah who must yet come?

How do Dominionists reject the idea that John was typological of another, future, real Elijah? You will not read any substantive explanation from them. In fact, other than Gentry, you will find little in Postmillennial literature about the Baptizer.

The real issue here however, is, to reiterate for emphasis:
☞ John was Elijah, per Jesus.
☞ John, as Elijah initiated the "restoration of all things."
☞ The restoration was to be completed at the Great Day of the Lord.
☞ John proclaimed the imminence of the Day of the Lord.
☞ It is, therefore, *prima facie* true that the completion of the restoration of all things was truly, objectively near in the first century.
☞ This means the end of the age judgment that John proclaimed was not, and could not be, a type or foreshadowing of another restoration of all things at the end of another age, totally unrelated to what John foretold.

Consider this about the admission that John was the fulfillment of the Elijah prophecy in Malachi. Gentry says John fulfilled that prophecy. Well, Elijah was to come before the Great Day of the Lord– the finalization of the restoration of all things.

Gentry and virtually all Dominionists have John coming as Elijah, but, then, they claim the restoration of all things initiated by John has not yet occurred. But wait, they say the Great Day of the Lord was AD 70. So, John, as Elijah, was ostensibly heralding and serving as a sign of two Great Days of the Lord. Of course, the question is, where is the textual justification for this?

John proclaimed *one* Day of the Lord. As the Voice in the Wilderness, he did not so much as mention two Days. He predicted the coming of the Lord in judgment and reward (Isaiah 40:10-11), when YHVH would make up the jewels of His crown (Malachi 3:15f).

So, Gentry and the postmillennialists say John was Elijah. He proclaimed the Great Day of the Lord. However, they say the consummation has not yet occurred. But, this creates a temporal disconnect. They are creating a two millennia gap between John, as the sign of the Great Day and the actual coming of the Day. This dishonors John's prediction that the Day was at hand.

> **Elijah was to come before the resurrection, the restoration of all things at the Great Day of the Lord.**
> **John was Elijah.**
> **This means John was the herald of the eschatological consummation of the work he personally initiated.**
> **He was not a type of another Elijah and the end he proclaimed was not a foreshadowing of a greater event.**

## Why AD 70 Was Not A Type of Another End of The Age

> **Reason #8 - Paul Said the Goal of All the Previous Ages Had Come in His Generation (1 Corinthians 10:11).**

I personally consider this point to be a fatal argument against the claim that AD 70 was a type of a yet future eschaton.

If the Dominionists– and all futurists– are correct in asserting that AD 70 was typological, including the arrival of the New Covenant creation, the Wedding, etc. then it means those events were not the Lord's ultimate eschatological goal. They were in fact "stop gap,"*interim* measures until the "real goal" finally comes. This is not what Paul said in 1 Corinthians.

Even on a cursory reading this passage is highly significant since Paul says the end of the ages had arrived. He very clearly was not saying the end of the Christian age had arrived. He was not saying *the end of time* had arrived, or else he was patently wrong. The question that needs to be asked is, the end of what age had arrived?

The Jews only believed in two ages and Jesus and the New Testament writers concurred. The Jews believed in "this age" and the "age to come." Their "this age" was the age of Moses and the Law and the "age to come" was the age of Messiah and the New Covenant. The age of Moses and the Law was to end, while the age of Messiah and the New Covenant was to be eternal. Given this view of the ages, it is patently false to interpret such passages as Matthew 24:2-3 as predictions or inquiries about the end of the Christian Age.[89]

---

[89] See my *We Shall Meet Him In The Air: The Wedding of the King of kings*, for a demonstration that the Olivet Discourse is concerned about one event: AD 70. The book is available on Kindle, from my websites, Amazon and

There are two Greek words we need to examine to help us appreciate 1 Corinthians 10:11. The first word is translated as "end," and is the word *tele*, from *telos*. This word can and often does mean termination, or end as we often think of it, e. g. "the end of all things has drawn near" (1 Peter 4:7).

However, this is not the whole story, even in 1 Peter 4. Even when the idea of termination is dominant, there is often another idea present and it is that the *goal* of what was being terminated pointed to and anticipated has been reached. (See the Lexicons for all the derivatives of *teleios*).

Thus, to say something was coming to an end, indicated *it had served its purpose and had now had reached its prophetic, destined goal.* Paul said Christ was "the end of the law for righteousness, to all those who believe" (Romans 10:4). Not only was Jesus the end of the Law objectively, since he brought the Old Covenant age to its end, but he was the *goal* of that Old World. As Galatians 3:23f says, the Law was a guardian of those under that System to bring them to Christ, and, "the faith." When that system of "the faith" was fully set in place, the Law was supposed to end. Thus, the end (*tele*) of the Law was not only the *termination* of the Law, but the *goal* of the Law.

For Paul to say therefore, that the end of the ages had arrived was an incredible statement! But, he did not stop with the word *tele*. He spoke of his contemporary brethren as those "upon whom the ends of the ages has come." When he said the end of the ages had *come*, he used another distinctive word. He uses the perfect tense of *katantao*. This word is used some twelve times in the New Testament. It means "to

---

other retailers.

69

arrive at something, to arrive at a destination"[90] This word is used, normally, to speak of arriving at a destination of travel.[91]

Four times *katantao* is used in a theological sense.

**First**, it is used by Paul when he says the twelve tribes were serving God night and day, hoping to "come" (or attain) unto the resurrection (Acts 26:7). Very clearly, resurrection was the prophetic goal or destiny of Israel's Messianic promises.

**Second**, Paul chided the Corinthians for being puffed up with pride. They thought of themselves as the "all in all" of Christianity and maturity. However, Paul asks the rhetorical question, Did the gospel come unto you only?" (1 Corinthians 14:36). This was Paul's way of saying they were not the goal of the preaching of the gospel. The gospel had other "destinations" beyond Corinth!

**Third**, *katantao* is used by the same apostle when he says the charismata were given to equip the church to do the work of the ministry "until we all come (*katantao*) to the unity of the faith, to the measure of the stature of the fullness of Christ" (Ephesians 4:13. The unity of the faith was the goal or destination anticipated by the praxis of the charismata. And, it was the arrival of the unity of the faith that would not only be the goal but the termination of the charismata (1 Corinthians 13:8f). Termination and goal go hand in hand here.

**Fourth,** in Philippians 3:11, Paul said it was his fervent desire and prayer to "attain" (*katantao*) to the resurrection from the dead. Just like resurrection was the goal of Israel's eschatological and Messianic aspirations, Paul, who preached nothing but the hope of Israel (Acts

---

[90] See Bauer's, *Arndt and Gingrich Greek Lexicon*, (University of Chicago Press, 1979)415.

[91] See for instance, Acts 16:1; 18:19, 24; 20:15; 21:7; 25:13; 27:12; 28:13

24; 25; 26; 28) said the resurrection was his desired goal. It was his desired destination.

With the use of *telos* and *katantao* then, Paul was undeniably saying that not only was the termination of the previous ages at hand, but *the goal of all previous ages was being achieved!* This has incredible implications.

## WHAT WAS THE GOAL OF THE AGES?

To see the implications of Paul's statement, we need to remind ourselves of the goal of the ages. What did all previous ages anticipate, predict and point toward? The answer can be couched in different terms.

The goal of the previous ages was the *New Creation* (Isaiah 65-66) and repeatedly, Paul said the New Creation was a reality in Christ: "If any man be in Christ, he is a new creation, old things are passed away, behold, all things are become new!" (2 Corinthians 5:17, see Ephesians 4; Colossians 3, etc.). As we observe in this work, the Dominionists agree the New Creation foretold in the Old Testament did "arrive" in AD 70.

The goal of the ages was *the Age to Come* (Luke 20:33f), when "this age" would come to an end (Matthew 13:39-40). Gentry, DeMar,

Mathison, McDurmon,[92] as we will demonstrate, all agree, "the age to come" arrived, at least in some way, in AD 70.

The destination of the previous ages was *the age of the resurrection* (Luke 20:33f), wherein sons of God would be produced by resurrection, (not by the marrying and giving in marriage like under the Old Covenant) and could never die. Repeatedly, Paul said believers were joined with Christ's death, burial and resurrection in baptism, raised to walk in newness of life, forgiven of sin and were thereby *sons of God by faith* (Galatians 3:26-28; Romans 6:3f; Colossians 2:11-13). He also said that now, in Christ, "there is no condemnation" (Romans 8:1f), as opposed to existence under the Law–his "This Age"-- where, "I was alive once, without the law, but the commandment came, sin revived, and I died" (Romans 7:7f). The then still present age of the Law was still the ministration of death (2 Corinthians 3:6f), but was, "nigh unto passing away"(Hebrews 8:13).

The goal of the previous ages was *the New Covenant World of the Messiah* (Galatians 3:23f). The Law was only a tutor, a guardian, of those under it, "until the Seed should come to whom the promises were made." It cannot be argued that the Law ended with the mere appearance of Jesus, for this would indicate the Law passed when He was born. The coming under consideration has to be His coming to fully establish the New Covenant and remove the Old.

---

[92] The "age to come" was a key point in my debate with McDurmon. He appealed to Luke 20 and Jesus' prediction of no marrying in the age to come. He said if preterists believe the age to come has arrived, we should disband our marriages. However, I noted from McDurmon's own book that he believes "the age to come" from Jesus' perspective was/ is *the Christian age*, and we are now living in "the age to come" anticipated by Jesus! Thus, per McDurmon's own position, he needs to disband his marriage! He offered no response to this.

72

The goal of all the previous ages and *God's eternal purpose*, was the arrival of the age in which, "He might gather together in one all things in Christ, both which are in heaven and which are on earth–in Him" (Ephesians 1:10). More on this momentarily. This was to be accomplished in the "fulness of times" and, as we know from Ephesians 2:11f, was being accomplished, not in a restoration of national Israel, but in the body of Christ, the church. We also know Jesus appeared in the fulness of time (Galatians 4:4. Therefore, the time for the goal of the ages to be realized had come with the advent of Christ.

The destination anticipated by the previous ages was, in a word, *the kingdom*. This is why our text is so important. It must be remembered at this juncture that the millennialist does not believe the Church age was anticipated by the previous ages. In fact, according to leading millennialists, the Church age, the age established by Jesus through his blood, and proclaimed by Paul, *was a total mystery to the previous ages!*

Pentecost says, "The existence of this present age which was to interrupt God's established program with Israel, was a mystery (Matthew 13:11).[93] He goes ahead to say the Church age was not foretold by the Old Testament prophets. He also adds, "The existence of an entirely new age which only interrupts temporarily God's program for Israel, is one of the strongest arguments for the premillennial position. It is necessary for one who rejects that interpretation to prove that the church itself is the consummation of God's program."(136). Finally, on page 137 of the same work, Pentecost says, "The concept must stand that this whole age with its program was not revealed in the Old Testament, but constitutes a new program and a new line of revelation in this present age....It has been

---

[93] Dwight Pentecost, *Things To Come*, (Grand Rapids, Zondervan, 1980)134+.

illustrated how this whole age existed in the mind of God without having been revealed in the Old Testament."

So, what we have is this: Paul said *the goal of the previous ages* had arrived. The destination anticipated by all previous ages was being reached. However, what was occurring when Paul wrote, the age that was breaking in, *was the Church age!* According to the millennialists the Kingdom age, *which is not the Church age*, is the goal of all the previous ages. However, since Paul said what was happening when he wrote was the goal of the previous ages, then the restoration of national Israel cannot be the goal of all previous ages. And of course, this means the millennial paradigm is fundamentally flawed.

If the Church age was the goal of the previous ages, then the church is not a "temporary interruption" of God's kingdom plans. It is undeniably true Paul says that what was happening in his day, through his ministry–and don't forget he proclaimed the "hope of Israel"–was in fact that goal. The church was the fulfillment of the "hope of Israel." It was the goal of all previous ages! Thus, the millennial doctrine is false.

When Paul says the goal of the previous ages had arrived, this has incredible application for the term "last days." It must be remembered that the kingdom, God's promise to Israel, was to be established in the last days (Isaiah 2:2). Paul of course, said the time of the end was near (1 Corinthians 7:26f; Philippians 4:5, etc.). Now, if Paul affirmed the nearness of the end and said the goal of the previous ages had arrived, this can only mean the last days foretold by the Old Testament prophets were present. Of course, the implications for the millennial view, given this reality, are staggering since they deny that Israel's last days were in existence after Matthew 12. However, Paul's statements are too clear to ignore. The end was near. The goal of the previous ages had arrived. This means Israel's last days were present when he wrote. This destroys the entire millennial house of cards.

74

Paul's statement in 1 Corinthians 10:11 also has implications for the Amillennial and Postmillennial views. Both of these paradigms insist the current Christian age will one day end, giving way to another "eternal" age to come.[94] This view is fundamentally flawed. It creates two "ages to come" and thus, two eschatological hopes, in direct contradiction to scripture. We will show how Postmillennialists actually admit that the Christian age is the "age to come" predicted by the OT prophets and arrived in AD 70. We will show that the OT prophets only foretold one eschatology, and had one hope. Thus, the Dominionist (and Amillennial) view of yet another "age to come" is pure fabrication.

Paul's use of two distinctive and significant words (*telos* and *katantao*), to speak of what was happening in his day is a powerful testimony to the place of the church in God's Scheme of Redemption. It is the blood bought Church of the Lord Jesus Christ that was and is the goal of the previous ages. This means the church was not to pass away with the dissolution of the Jewish Aeon, as some suggest.

Would it not be strange indeed if *the goal of the previous ages* endured for only 40 years? Is that what God had in mind for the "kingdom that shall never pass away"? To suggest the church was to pass away after 40 years surely indicates that God could not be through with the "goal of the ages" quick enough, so He could get to... what? *What other goal of the previous ages is there in Scripture?*

It appears to me that those who are suggesting the church was to cease at the parousia are positing just a modified form of the millennial view: the church really is not the "consummation of God's program."

Unless one can demonstrate that Paul had something other than the Church, the body of Christ in mind when he spoke of the goal of the

---

[94] Of course, as we have shown, the current kingdom of Christ– the current age– is eternal and it was the goal of the previous ages.

ages, then *the Church was the anticipated destiny of the previous ages.* This destroys the millennial doctrine that the church is a "temporary interruption" of God's kingdom plan. Take another look at Pentecost's comments just above. He says the strongest argument for the premillennial view is the idea the church was not "the consummation of God's program." Well, unless Paul had something other than the church in mind when he said the goal of the ages had arrived, then 1 Corinthians 10:11 proves beyond doubt the church really is "the consummation of God's program," and that being so, millennialism is falsified.

Unless one can demonstrate Paul had some other destiny, some other goal of the ages in mind different from the Church, there is not, nor was there, another destiny of the ages other than the Church. This means that what had broken into the Old World, the New Creation, was about to be perfected, manifested, vindicated and glorified, not terminated.

The body of Christ was the eternal purpose of God and the goal of the previous ages. Any doctrine that disparages or depreciates the value, the honor and the glory of the church is a Christ dishonoring doctrine. Further, it flies in the face of Paul's statement that the Church was, and is, the goal of all previous ages.

I must interject a few additional thoughts here as they relate to "the goal of the ages." Paul was firm, there was but "one hope" (Ephesians 4:4) and that one hope was nothing but the anticipation of the imminent fulfillment of God's Old Covenant promises made to Israel, found in Moses and the prophets.

In my debate with McDurmon I continually emphasized this critical issue. Hebrews 11 says from Creation onward there was but one eschatological goal- the "better resurrection" (11:35). That one hope ran through all of the OT worthies and was to be consummated in "Zion" the locus of the end of the millennium resurrection (Isaiah 25:6f).

76

McDurmon, while giving lip service to the reality of "one hope" nonetheless said the real, "final" hope was *not* related to the fulfillment of God's OT promises to Israel, but will only be fulfilled at the end of the current Christian age when Genesis is fulfilled. The events of AD 70 foreshadow the real, "final" fulfillment of the eschatological "one hope." This is an overt rejection of the Biblical testimony.

This flies in the face of Paul's inspired affirmation that the "goal of the ages has arrived." If the goal of the ages had arrived– and was about to be shortly revealed and vindicated at the parousia-- then it is specious to say the goal of the ages was a mere type of true goal of the ages, at the consummation of a totally different age.

Paul said the goal of the previous ages had arrived. Dominionists say the "real" goal had not arrived.

The Dominionists are in direct opposition to Paul and inspiration.

This is *prima facie* falsification of the idea that what was happening in the first century was a type or foreshadowing of the true goal to be arrived at, at the consummation of another age.

## Why AD 70 Was Not A Type of Another End of the Age

> **Reason #9 - Then Comes The End, When He Shall Deliver The Kingdom To the Father - The End Was In AD 70!**

"But each one in his own order: Christ the first fruits, afterward those who are Christ's at His coming. Then comes the end, when He delivers the kingdom to God the Father, when He puts an end to all rule and all authority and power. For He must reign till He has put all enemies under His feet. The last enemy that will be destroyed is death. For "He has put all things under His feet."But when He says "all things are put under Him," it is evident that He who put all things under Him is excepted. Now when all things are made subject to Him, then the Son Himself will also be subject to Him who put all things under Him, that God may be all in all" (1 Corinthians 15:23-28).

Few, if any, futurist commentators posit "the end" of 1 Corinthians 15:24f as anything but the end of the Christian age– the "final end." They see "the end" as the termination of Christ's rule on the throne. This is so widely accepted I will not take the time to document it with extensive quotes.[95] Until the advent of the modern Dominionist theology, no one suggested "the end" had "a fulfillment" in AD 70, which was in Paul's mind preliminary to "the real end."

---

[95] A single example of many that could be given is that of Seriah: "Christ's reign is perpetual during this age (and will end when this age does). (1999, 47, n. 9). Seriah equates the "eternal" reign of Christ with the "perpetual" things of the Old Covenant. He rightly notes that in the OT, many things were "eternal" yet destined to end, at the Divinely appointed time. What he clearly overlooks is that scripture says Christ's rule / throne / kingdom has "no end." This is totally different.

79

Of course, the question under review here is whether Paul anticipated a preliminary, typological "the end" pointing to the "real," real end, or, whether he believed "the 'real' end" was truly in view.

The term "the end" is used 19 times in the NT, (NKJV) from Romans - Revelation. Paul speaks of death being "the end" of sin (Romans 6:21-22). Christ is "the end of the law" (Romans 10:4; cf. 2 Corinthians 3:13, where Moses could not see "the end" of Torah). In Revelation, God is "the first and the last, the beginning and the end" (1:8; 22:13).

In the majority of occurrences there are definite eschatological overtones to the context. This is especially true in Hebrews (3:6, 14; 6:11; 9:26) as well as James (5:11) and 1 Peter (1:9; 4:7; 4:17).

"The end" in 1 Corinthians also has definite eschatological connections.

1 Corinthians 1:4-8– The Corinthians possessed the charismatic gifts. Those gifts had confirmed them and those gifts would continue to confirm them "until the end," the Day of the Lord.

1 Corinthians 10:11 – The end of the ages, i.e. the goal of the previous ages, was even then falling on them. As we have seen, the consummative nature of this end of the age cannot, in any sense, be labeled as a mere type. It is in fact, contrasted with the Old Testament events that were typological, but, *those types* pointed to Paul's generation.[96]

---

[96] While the specific term "the end" does not appear in other texts in 1 Corinthians, the eschatological consummation is nonetheless present. In chapter 7, Paul said "the time has been shortened" echoing Jesus' words in Matthew 24:21-27. He said "the fashion of this world is passing away." Similarly, the apostle anticipated the cessation of the charismata at the arrival of "that which is perfect" (1

When we come to "the end" in 1 Corinthians 15 there is no contextual reason whatsoever to delineate between the anticipated end there and that mentioned earlier in the epistle. Remember that McDurmon agreed there was in fact a fulfillment of "the end" of 1 Corinthians 15, in AD 70. This admission nullifies any other, future fulfillment.

Several factors militate against defining "the end" in 1 Corinthians 15 as a referent to the end of time, or the end of the Christian age.

### Fulfillment of the Hope of Israel

**Fact #1** - The end under consideration is the time of the fulfillment of God's Old Covenant promises made to Israel. As we have shown, there is but one eschatological hope in scripture. The eschatology of Genesis and God's promises to Abraham are conflated with the promises of Israel. Fulfillment is posited at the end of Israel's history. Hebrews 11 proves this definitively, by showing the one eschatological hope encompassed Abel, Enoch, Noah, Abraham, to Moses and consummated at Zion.[97]

---

Corinthians 13:8f). This hearkens back to chapter 1:4-8 where he said the Corinthians would possess the gifts until "the end," the Day of the Lord. So, again, while the term "the end" is not used extensively, there is no evidence to support the idea Paul had two ends in mind.

[97] The One Hope and Zion were central points in my debate with McDurmon. He sought desperately to delineate between Genesis eschatology, which he equated with Abrahamic eschatology and the promises made to Israel. This is why he argued that the Genesis / Abrahamic promises are yet future, even though there was a typological fulfillment of those promises (i.e. Israel's promises) in AD 70. In other words, for McDurmon and the Dominionists, the fulfillment of Israel's promises in AD 70 foreshadow the yet future fulfillment of Edenic / Abrahamic promises. As I demonstrated repeatedly, Hebrews 11 negates any attempt to distinguish

Galatians 3 discusses the Abrahamic promises. Paul makes sure to say Abraham's promises were not to be fulfilled under or through Torah, for then they would not be promises of faith and grace. However, those promises were to be fulfilled when "the faith" i.e. the New Covenant of faith and grace, would arrive (3:23-24).

In 1 Corinthians 15, Paul draws from Genesis (v. 22) and the prophecies of Israel in his discussion of the resurrection. He has one resurrection, one hope in focus. Fulfillment of the Edenic promises– and thus, fulfillment of the *Abrahamic promises*– would be when Isaiah 25 and Hosea 13 would be fulfilled.

This point is particularly troublesome for Amillennialists and Postmillennialists who believe God's Old Covenant relationship with Israel was terminated in the first century. If God was through with Israel in the first century, how can His *covenant promises* to her remain valid until the "end of the Christian age"? If His covenant promises to Israel remain valid, they remain His covenant people. This is inescapable.

Incredibly, in the lead up to my debate with McDurmon, I asked him: "At what point of time, and in what event (events) were (or will) *all* (not just some, or most) but *all*, of God's Old Covenant promises, made to Old Covenant Israel after the flesh, be completely fulfilled, (fully accomplished) and His Covenant relationship with her terminated / consummated?" Joel responded, "The short answer to what you're getting at is: the physical, bodily resurrection of the dead."

This is just *stunning*. On the one hand, Dominionists argue, strongly, against the Dispensationalists who claim that Israel remains God's covenant people. (Remember how DeMar claims all of God's Old Covenant promises to Israel are fulfilled). On the other hand,

---

between Edenic / Abrahamic eschatology and the promises made to Israel.

McDumon says Israel will remain God's covenant people until "the physical, bodily resurrection of the dead."

McDurmon is patently wrong. Paul said Torah and Old Covenant Israel were about to be cast out for persecuting the New Covenant Seed (Galatians 4:22f).[98] So, Torah and Israel were about to be cast out, for persecuting the church in the first century. Yet, somehow, God's covenant and *His covenant relationship with them*, will remain until "the physical, bodily resurrection of the dead" at the end of human history!

The point is, Paul never looks beyond the fulfillment of God's promises to Old Covenant Israel in his discussion of the resurrection. This is exceedingly strange if in fact he taught the resurrection would be the fulfillment of New Covenant promises at the end of the New Covenant age.

**"The End" Is The End of Torah**
**Fact #2** - Not only does Paul see the resurrection as the fulfillment of God's Old Covenant promises made to Israel, he posits fulfillment at the end of that covenant history. The apostle says the resurrection would be when sin, "the sting of death," and when "the law" that is the "strength of sin" would be overcome and removed (v. 55-56).

Numerous times in my debate with McDurmon, (and in numerous formal debates), I noted that in scripture only one law is ever described as "the strength of sin" and that was Torah, the Law of Moses (cf. Romans 7; 2 Corinthians 3, Galatians 2-3, etc.). *McDurmon never denied this* and in the majority of my debates, when

---

[98] See my book, *In Flaming Fire*, for a demonstration that in 2 Thessalonians 1:4ff Paul anticipated Israel's expulsion at the imminent parousia, for persecuting the New Covenant Seed. 2 Thessalonians is emphatic and undeniable in positing the termination of God's covenant with Israel at the parousia in the lifetime of the first century Thessalonians.

I have asked my opponent to define "the law" that was the "strength of sin" they have answered, "The law of Moses."[99] So, take a look at what this means.

**The resurrection– resurrection from the Adamic death– would be when "the law" that was the "strength of sin" was overcome and removed.**

**"The law" that was the "strength of sin" was the Law of Moses, Torah.**

**Therefore, the resurrection– resurrection from the Adamic death– would be when "the law" that was the "strength of sin" was overcome and removed.**

Very clearly then, unless one is willing to say the Law of Moses remains valid today the resurrection from the Adamic death has been fulfilled. And remember, virtually no eschatological paradigm openly says Torah is still valid, in spite of McDurmon's quote above.[100]

---

[99] In a recent (2012) written debate, my Amillennial opponent, Jerry McDonald responded with this definition. When I noted the consequences of this (true) answer, i.e. the resurrection would therefore be at the end of the Law of Moses, McDonald began some of the most desperate verbiage imaginable, changing positions several times. That debate is archived on my websites.

[100] The mass confusion of Dominionism is manifest in regard to the Law of Moses. On the one hand they say the Law remains valid– this is essential to their Dominion theology. Yet, they tell us all of the ceremonies, sacrifices and cultic praxis and Sabbaths have been removed! But, they do not believe the things foreshadowed in those ceremonies and Sabbaths have been fulfilled. For instance, the eternal rest of resurrection salvation typified in the Sabbaths, remains unfulfilled per McDurmon, Gentry, Bahnsen, et. al. So, per the

This logically demands "the end" of 1 Corinthians 15 is the end of the Old Covenant age of Israel, the end of Torah. It is not the end of time; it is not the end of the Christian age. Since 1 Corinthians 15 is patently about the "final" resurrection, not a type or shadow of another one, this definitively falsifies the claim that AD 70 was a type of the real end.

### The End as the Wedding

**Fact #4** - Virtually all commentators agree "the end" of 1 Corinthians 15 is the time of Christ's coming for his Wedding. I discuss the Wedding motif later in this work, so I will forego an in-depth discussion here. I will simply take note of a few critical issues.

Paul said Christ would *present* the church to himself (Ephesians 5:25f). I have consulted over 50 commentators and everyone of them agrees that the presentation occurs at the parousia, agreeing with Matthew 25:1f; Rev. 19:6f.

So, here, in a nutshell, is the problem for the Postmillennial (and Amillennial) world.

**Christ's coming in 1 Corinthians 15, at the final "the end" (being the same end / coming as in Matthew 25:31f; 1 Thessalonians 4, Rev. 19, etc.) is when he surrenders, abdicates,**

---

Dominionists Jesus' words "not one jot or one tittle shall pass from the law until it is all fulfilled" *really* meant that some– *a lot!–* of jots and tittles of the law would (have) pass *without being fulfilled*. I challenged McDurmon to explain how anyone could get that idea from Jesus' words, but he never responded.

his throne[101] – giving it to the Father– (Amillennialism, Postmillennialism).

**But, the coming in 1 Corinthians 15, (Matthew 25, Rev. 19, etc.) is the time of Christ's wedding.**

**Therefore, at his coming for his wedding, Christ divorces, i.e. surrenders his wife. He hands her over to the Father, is no longer married to her.**

Let's be honest here. *No one* says Jesus will *divorce his Bride* at his parousia. And yet, if the traditional claim that "the end" is when he surrenders the kingdom is true, then Jesus must divorce his Bride at the very moment he is to present her to himself! This is one of those huge disparities, one of the major self contradictions within Christian doctrine that simply has not been addressed. There is no reconciling these two positions.

The application here should be evident. Gentry says the wedding of Matthew 25 is the consummative, true end, not a typological Wedding or end. Likewise, he says 1 Corinthians 15, "the end," is the time of the Wedding of Matthew 25. Yet, he then says Christ married his bride in AD 70, with the New Covenant Bride fully supplanting the Old Bride. And of course, he says AD 70 was typological of the true end! Mathison seemingly agrees with this assessment, claiming Matthew 25 predicts the yet future parousia (1995, 144). Yet, he says the wedding of Revelation 21 is "being fulfilled." I fail to see how a wedding can continue for 2000 years!

Thus, of logical necessity, Gentry creates a doctrine of two weddings, two Brides (?) and most assuredly two comings. McDurmon hints at

---

[101] Mathison says, "Paul teaches that on the Last Day, Christ gives the kingdom over to the Father (1 Corinthians 15:24). The last days is not the day Christ receives the kingdom; it is the day when the kingdom is consummated." (*Hope*, 1999, 179)

two Brides / Weddings, or is it two Grooms?, in his comments on Matthew 25. He applies the parable to AD 70 and the Jews: "They had missed their opportunity, not having their lamps lit. They lost all future inheritance, and were left no better than adulterers, *as far as that particular Bridegroom was concerned"* (2011, 29). My emphasis,

The position these men take demands either two weddings, two Brides, or two Grooms. They claim AD 70 was the wedding of Christ, the divorce of the Old Covenant, unfaithful bride. Well, if that was typological of the real end, we have every right to conclude that the church will one day be divorced for unfaithfulness and Jesus will marry another bride, under a (another) new covenant. This is a loathable idea.

The problem is, if "the end" of 1 Corinthians 15 is the "real" end and if it is the time of the Wedding of Christ, the Biblical truth is there was but *one* wedding foretold (Isaiah 62; Hosea 1:10f; 2:18f) at the end of the Old Covenant age, at the fall of Jerusalem (Matthew 22:1-10).[102] That leads us to this:

**The end of 1 Corinthians 15:24-25 is the consummative end, not a typological "end."**

**The end of 1 Corinthians 15:24-25 is the time of the parousia of Christ for his *wedding*.**

**The coming of Christ for his wedding was in AD 70 at the destruction of Jerusalem (Matthew 22; Revelation 19– Gentry, DeMar, McDurmon, Mathison (1999, 157f).**

---

[102] See my development of the Wedding promises to Israel in my *Who Is This Babylon?* There is no scriptural justification whatsoever for the idea that the Wedding of AD 70 anticipated another Wedding.

**Therefore, the end of 1 Corinthians 15, the consummative end, was in AD 70, at the destruction of Jerusalem.**

There is no logical, textual way to posit the wedding (not the betrothal) in AD 70 and yet, posit the wedding at the so called "real end."

## The End as the Harvest
**Fact #5** - Christ the first fruit of the Harvest

Christ is "the first fruit." There is "each in his own order" (Greek *tagma*, meaning in order of occurrence). "Those that are Christ's at his coming, "then comes the end." Very clearly, in 1 Corinthians 15 "the end" is the climax of the harvest. While a great deal could be said of this, we will be brief simply presenting more of the Dominionist self contradictions and problems with the motif of the harvest and AD 70.

As with other eschatological motifs and passages, the Dominionists differ strongly about the application of the harvest motif. Gentry applies Matthew 13 to the climax of human history, (2003,140) and says it teaches there will be no more days after the "end of the age" of Matthew 13:39f.[103]

Revelation 14 likewise discusses the harvest of the earth (land). Although he does not comment specifically on the harvest motif,

---

[103] Gentry says of the "end of the age" in Matthew 13, "Matthew uses *sunteleia* (which appears in the phrase 'the end of the age' only for the end of the world's end: Matthew 13:39, 40, 49; 24:3; 28:20." *(The Olivet Discourse Made Easy*, (Draper, Va., Apologetics Group, 2010)46, n. 7). This is patently false. In Matthew 24:3 the disciples were not asking about the end of human history, as Gentry himself admits.

Gentry, definitely posits the fulfillment of Revelation 14 during the Jewish War,[104]

In stark contrast with Gentry and Mathison, Leithhart says: "Jesus' parable of the tares has been interpreted for centuries as a parable about the church age, but it makes much better sense as a parabolic description of the post-exilic history of Israel. With the return from exile, Yahweh sowed the land with the seed of man and beast, but since that time Satan has been busy sowing tares among the wheat. Jesus has now come with His winnowing fork, and before the end of the age, the wheat and tares will be separated. The end of the age thus refers not to the final judgment but to the close of 'this generation.'"[105] DeMar concurs (*Madness*, 1994, 155). And McDurmon, as we have seen, says Matthew 13: "Describes the then soon coming end of that old age and the destruction of its children, and the beginning of the gathering in of the true children of God's kingdom. It should not be understood as teaching anything beyond this."(2011,49) As we have noted, McDurmon is wrong to see the end of the age as the beginning of the harvest. It is, as seen just above, the completion of the harvest of the Old Covenant world, as Leithart says.[106]

---

[104] Kenneth Gentry, *Before Jerusalem Fell*, (Fountain Inn, SC., Victorious Hope Publishing, 2010)244+

[105] Peter Leithart, *The Promise of His Coming*, (Moscow, Idaho, Canon Press, 2004)95.

[106] This is really quite a critical, but under emphasized point. The harvest is the climax of the Old Covenant age and the gathering of those who had lived under that aeon, including those in Hebrews 11. The harvest was *the judgment of that Old World*, for its inefficiency and failure. But, it was likewise the full establishment of the unending kingdom / age of the kingdom. There will never be an end / harvest of the New Covenant age. This simply means, as we have noted, "of the increase of his government, there shall be no end."

Let me make a point here:
The harvest of 1 Corinthians 15 is the harvest of Matthew 13. If not, why not? Was Jesus the first fruit of two harvests, at the end of two different ages and two different parousias? No, there was but "one hope" in scripture, and from John, who announced the imminence of the harvest, to Revelation, the pronouncement was the time had come for the harvest.

The harvest of Matthew 13 occurred in AD 70 and there is no further application – McDurmon.

Therefore, the harvest of 1 Corinthians 15 was in AD 70 and there is no further application.

This conclusion is confirmed by the indisputable fact of Jesus being the "first born" or "first fruit" of the resurrection. Acts 26:21f says Jesus was "the first to be raised from the dead." This is hugely problematic for those insisting that "the end" of 1 Corinthians 15 must be the end of human history, climaxing in a resurrection of human corpses out of the dirt.

Gentry sees a problem and attempts to escape the force of it by saying: "Jesus is called the first born, yet we know that others physically arose from the dead prior to Him, some during his ministry. Thus, his resurrection was of a different order, a different order that made him a "first' in that respect." (1992, 283-284). You will note Gentry fails to define or explain this "different order." It seems obvious he was simply trying to evade the force of Jesus being the first to be raised from the dead, yet clearly not the first to be raised from physical death. Gentry's presuppositional view of the nature of Adamic Death and the resurrection prevents him from accepting Jesus as the first to be raised from Adamic Death (defined as biological death). This is an insurmountable problem for those defining Adamic Death as biological death.

Paul's use of harvest imagery and description of Jesus as the first fruit demands that the time of harvest was present in the first century. And undeniably, in 1 Corinthians 15 the "end" is the *consummation* of the harvest initiated by Jesus as the first fruit. This was the "final" end of the age harvest. It did not point to another harvest, at another end. This falsifies the claim that there was "a fulfilment" of 1 Corinthians 15 but, we are still looking for the "final" fulfillment.

**Fact #6 - When He Delivers the Kingdom– This Is Not Abdication!**
As we noted above, one of, if not the *key,* presuppositions about "the end" in 1 Corinthians 15 is that it is the end of time and the physical resurrection. Since, it is reasoned, Corinthians is about a physical resurrection, and since that has not occurred, then clearly, "the end" has not come. Of course, this is purely presuppositional and what we have presented above falsifies it.

Another foundational presupposition is directly related. And that is "the end" is *the end of Christ's rule* on his throne, when he supposedly "surrenders" the throne, handing it over to the Father and thus, terminating his royal regency. This is based on the word *paradidoi* in v. 24 rendered "delivers."[107] Wayne Jackson argues: "Now, remember that according to verse 24, when He comes again, He will no longer be reigning, because He will have delivered the kingdom back to the Father."[108]

This is unwarranted linguistically and contextually. Let me make just a couple of very quick points and urge you to read my other comments later in this work, as they relate to the wedding motif.

---

[107] *Paradidoi can* mean to "surrender" in some contexts. However, in 1 Corinthians 15, Paul said he had *delivered* the gospel to the Corinthians and clearly does not mean he "surrendered" the gospel or his authority over it.

[108] Wayne Jackson, *The AD 70 Theory*, (Stockton, CA. Courier Publications, 1990)37.

**First point** - If there was a typological fulfillment of 1 Corinthians 15 in AD 70– and if deliver means surrender or abdicate-- just exactly how did Jesus in any way abdicate the kingdom in AD 70? It is surely wrong to posit a typological fulfillment in AD 70 and yet, then claim that after all, there was no fulfillment of what was being foreshadowed! Thus, the argument that AD 70 was typological of the "real end" demands that in some way, in some manner, Christ abdicated his rule, his throne, and, divorced his wife! Just how do we see that depicted, in any manner whatsoever, in AD 70?

You will not find a Dominionist who describes AD 70 as in any way at all a typological abdication of the kingdom by Jesus. Just the opposite. Virtually all postmillennialists I have read speak of Jesus' coming in power and great glory. They speak of Christ exercising his Sovereignty. They speak of him being revealed as Messiah, sitting at the right hand of the Majesty (Gentry, DeMar, McDurmon, etc.).[109]

So, how can the postmillennialists strongly affirm that AD 70 was a sign of the full establishment of Jesus' throne and yet claim that somehow, someway, it foreshadows the abdication of that throne? This is just not sound logic, or theology. How exactly does enthronement typify abdication?

**Point #2** - You cannot interpret or define *paradidoi* in such a way as to contradict the Wedding motif. If, as we have seen, AD 70 is posited as the time of Jesus' wedding– *and virtually all Dominionists do*– then to say *1* Corinthians 15 demands abdication, thereby demands that

---

[109] There is strong linguistic support for the idea that AD 70 was the *sign* of Jesus' full entrance into his kingdom. Jeffrey A. Gibbs, *Jerusalem and Parousia*, (St. Louis, MO, Concordia Academic Press, 2000)198f– shows that "the sign of the Son of Man in heaven" is not a sign in the sky, but, that "the fall of Jerusalem was the sign of Christ's enthronement in the heavens." DeMar (1994, 158), Mathison (1999, 114), Gentry (1992, 274), Seriah, 1991, 173), etc.

Christ divorces his wife at the "real end." This is clearly a terrible suggestion.

**Point #3** - You cannot interpret the *end* in 1 Corinthians 15 in such a way as to contradict the harvest motif which linguistically and contextually demands that the "full end" of the harvest was near.

John taught the imminence of the harvest (Matthew 3). Jesus taught the nearness of the harvest (John 4:35). Jesus himself was the first fruit of the harvest, demanding the initiation of the harvest. Revelation says the harvest was near in the judgment of Babylon, which, incidentally, virtually all Dominionists identify as Old Covenant Jerusalem.

**Fact #7 - That God May Be All In All– The Fulfillment of Zechariah 14**

For brevity let me summarize some of the salient points of Zechariah 14.

✠We have the Day of the Lord, when He comes with all of His saints (v. 5).

✠It is the Day of the salvation of the remnant (Zechariah 13:8f).

✠It is the Day that a fountain of life giving water flows from Jerusalem. Needless to say, this is one of the sources for the prophecy of Revelation 21-22, the "post-millennial New Creation" i.e. the consummative end!

✠ It is the time when the feast of Tabernacles– which typified resurrection / harvest-- would be celebrated– i.e. when the resurrection would be memorialized and celebrated.

✠It would be the Day when "there shall be one King in all the earth" and in that Day "the Lord is One and His name One" (v. 9).

✠ It would be when the Lord came in judgment of the Old Covenant Jerusalem (v. 1-2).

We thus have in Zechariah a "thumbnail sketch" of 1 Corinthians 15 and Revelation 20-22![110] Now, if, as a host of scholars believe, Zechariah 14 is the source of Paul's prediction of the time when God would be "all in all" then the indisputable fact that Zechariah foretold the AD 70 judgment of Jerusalem– including resurrection predictions– positively identifies not only Zechariah, but, 1 Corinthians 15 as the definitive, final Day of the Lord.

So, here is what we have discovered about "the end" in 1 Corinthians 15:
✔It would be the time of the fulfillment of Israel's Old Covenant promises.
✔It would occur at the end of Torah, the law that was the strength of sin. (This logically and prophetically demands the establishment of the New Covenant).
✔It would be the time of Christ's wedding when, as most Dominionists agree, would likewise be when Christ divorced the Old Covenant unfaithful, harlot bride.
✔It would be at the consummation of the harvest, of which Christ was the first fruit.
✔ It would be when God became "all in all" in fulfillment of Zechariah 14.

Not one of these tenets allows us to see AD 70 as typological of the "real" end. There is no Biblical basis for that doctrine. It is a theological invention without merit.

---

[110] See my *Who Is This Babylon?* for a fuller discussion of Zechariah 14 and its influence on Revelation 20-22.

"The End" of 1 Corinthians 15 is the "final," consummative end– as virtually all commentators agree.

1 Corinthians 15 cannot be the end of time.

It cannot be the end of the Christian age.

It cannot be the end of Christ's enthronement "The End" of 1 Corinthians 15 is contextually defined as the climactic termination of the age of Torah, the Law that was the "strength of sin"– And this was in AD 70

Therefore, AD 70 was the final, consummative "the end" and not a type or shadow of the "real" end.

---

**Reason #10 - Ephesians 1:10 - "That in the stewardship of the fulness of time He would gather together all things in one body, in Christ."**

---

"Blessed be the God and Father of our Lord Jesus Christ, who has blessed us with every spiritual blessing in the heavenly places in Christ, just as He chose us in Him before the foundation of the world, that we should be holy and without blame before Him in love, having predestined us to adoption as sons by Jesus Christ to Himself, according to the good pleasure of His will, to the praise of the glory of His grace, by which He made us accepted in the Beloved. In Him we have redemption through His blood, the forgiveness of sins, according to the riches of His grace which He made to abound toward us in all wisdom and prudence, having made known to us the mystery of His will, according to His good pleasure which He purposed in Himself, that in the dispensation of the fullness of the times He might gather together in one all things in Christ, both which are in heaven and which are on earth—in Him" (Ephesians 1:3-10).

In this, Paul's longest sentence declaring God's marvelous scheme of Redemption, he affirms several things.

☛ His plan was determined before the foundation of the world.
☛ His plan was to reunite heaven and earth. This is patently the solution to the Adamic Curse.
☛ It was His plan to accomplish His purpose "in Christ."
☛ His purpose was to accomplish the reunification "in the stewardship of the fulness of time."

Very clearly, the reuniting of heaven and earth and the bringing together of all things, is nothing other than the restoration of all things which we have examined.[111] But, we want to focus on the clear delineation from Paul's pen as to when that reunification was to take place.

I consider it axiomatic that if God's eternal purpose, conceived before time, was focused on fulfillment at a given time, then it is *prima facie* proof that the fulfillment of that eternal purpose at the divinely appointed time (*kairos*) would not be indicative of another, greater, eternal purpose to gather together all things in Christ at another "fulness of time." In other words, in Ephesians 1 there is simply no way to claim Paul was discussing the work of Christ in the church as being typological.

Paul does not suggest in any way whatsoever that what he is discussing was an interim, typological work of God. After all, in Paul's eschatology and theology, it was the (typological) Mosaic Covenant that was "interim" between the fulfillment of the Abrahamic Covenant promises and fulfillment in Christ (Galatians 3:23-29). The church is not, in spite of the Dispensational claims to the contrary, God's interim plan. In Paul's theology, fulfillment of those Abrahamic promises was to take place at the end of that interim, typological age of Moses.

---

[111] Dominionists agree that Ephesians 1 is the "final" eschatological event. DeMar says: "We learn that the end relates to Jesus' 'summing up of all things... things that are in heavens and things upon the earth' takes place 'at His coming' when 'He delivers up the kingdom to God and the Father, when He has abolished all rule and all authority and power." (*End Times Fiction*, Nashville, Thomas Nelson, 2001)213.

97

> The only "interim" age, was the age of types and shadows, the Mosaic Covenant Age. That age stood between the Edenic and Abrahamic (resurrection) promises and the fulfillment of those promises in Christ. Those Edenic and Abrahamic promises were carried through and foreshadowed under Torah (cf. Hebrews 11) pointing toward fulfillment, not toward the establishment of another age of more types and shadows to be fulfilled at the termination of the age established by Christ.

But note Paul claims God's eternal, ultimate purpose was to be accomplished "in the fulness of time." It is mandatory to see he does not say the work would be *initiated* in the fulness of time and consummated at another fulness of time, or at the end of another age. That consummative work was to be accomplished, perfected, consummated "in the fulness of time."

Paul said it was God's eternal purpose to accomplish the foreordained reunification "in the fulness of *time*." The word translated as "time" is from *kairos* and is distinct from *chronos*, which means time generically. *Kairos* is the "divinely appointed time." It is the specific, appointed time determined by God for the accomplishment of His purpose (cf. Acts 17:30-31).

*Kairos* is an important word in the NT, particularly significant in the study of eschatology.[112] Invariably, the NT writers tell us the anticipated, prophesied time had arrived in their first century generation. *Kairos* is thus worthy of its own in-depth study. But we

---

[112] According to my count, *kairos* is used 82 times in the NT and its use in eschatological texts bears strong witness to the undeniable imminence of the end.

98

will not do that here. We will list a very few of the texts wherein *kairos* clearly designates a divinely appointed, special time.

❖ Matthew 8:29 - The "legion" of demons asked Jesus if he had come to torment them "before the time" (*kairos*). Very clearly, the demons realized there was a time appointed for their judgment.

❖ Matthew 16:3 - Jesus castigated the Jews for not recognizing "the signs of the times."

❖ - Matthew 26:18 - Jesus said his time, the appointed time for his passion, had arrived (cf. John 7:6, 8).

❖ - Luke 19:44 - Jesus lamented that Jerusalem did not recognize the time of her visitation.

❖ - Romans 3:26 - Paul said it was determined to proclaim Christ. and his message "at this time." The contrast is between Paul's present time and the past when God had "overlooked" man's sin. Note also that Christ died "in due time" (Romans 5:6).

❖ - Romans 8:18 - See just below. Paul spoke of the very real, very contemporary suffering (from *pathemata*, a word used almost exclusively of suffering for the name of Christ. It is not the suffering of the "human experience").

The suffering of "this present time" is the suffering Jesus predicted in Matthew 24 where he predicted his followers would suffer for his name in that generation. It is the persecution of Matthew 23:34, that Jesus predicted for his generation in the context of filling the measure of suffering.

Much more could be said of *kairos*, but this should suffice. It is clearly a word designating a divinely appointed time and the NT writers are unambiguous. They believed the divinely appointed time for the fulfillment of God's eschatological plan had arrived and was about to be fulfilled: "the time has come for the judgment" (1 Peter 4:17); "the time (*kairos*) is at hand" (Revelation 1:3).

In the Old Testament God foretold the "last days" as the time for the kingdom, the judgment and the resurrection. Thus, the "last days"[113] were the divinely appointed days, the *kairos*, for the accomplishment of His purposes– the reuniting of heaven and earth.

Take note of the message of Jesus (and John) in regard to the kingdom: "The time (*kairos*) is fulfilled, the kingdom of heaven is at hand" (literally, has drawn near). F. F. Bruce commented on the significance of Jesus' message: "These words express, among other things, the assurance that an ardently desired new order, long since foretold and awaited. was now on the point of realization."[114]

Gentry concurs: "Christ asserts 'the time is fulfilled.' What is 'the time' to which he refers? The Greek term here is *kairos*, which indicates 'the fateful and decisive point' that is ordained by God.' This 'time' surely refers to the prophetically anticipated time, the time of the coming of David's greater Son to establish the kingdom, for he immediately adds: 'the kingdom of *God* is at hand.'" (2009, 218). Gentry clearly does not grasp the significance of his admission, as few futurists commentators do.

Now, it is easy to expose the Dominionist self contradictions in regard to *kairos*– the divinely appointed time. Gentry and virtually all postmillennialists dichotomize between the appointed time of the first century from their hypothesized appointed time of the "real" end of the age. But, there is no such delineation in scripture. And what is so

---

[113] See my *The Last Days Identified*, for an in-depth discussion of the last days. The book is available from Amazon, my websites, Kindle and other retailers.

[114] F. F. Bruce, *The Time is Fulfilled*, (Exeter, Paternoster Press, 1978)15:

interesting is that the different representatives of the Dominionist paradigm actually bear witness to this.[115]

Romans 8:18f is considered by most scholars to be a prediction of the true end, the end of human history. But, notice some quotes from some of the leading postmillennialists in regard to this text and the "time" of fulfillment.

Demar says of Romans 8: "The New American Standard translation does not catch the full meaning of this passage. Following Robert Young's Literal Translation of the Bible, we read, 'For I reckon that the sufferings of the present time are not worthy to be compared with the glory about to be revealed in us.' Whatever the glory is, it was 'about to be revealed' (see Revelation 2:10; 3:2, 10; 10:4; 12:4; 17:8). Peter tells his readers that the 'Spirit of glory and of Christ rests on you' (1 Peter 4:14). This was a present condition, not something the people in Peter's day would have to wait for a future rapture." (1994, 191). So, according to DeMar, the fulfillment of Romans 8 was at hand in the first century.

This is not the dominant view in the Dominionist world. However, while it may not be the majority view, even McDurmon, who posits

---

[115] Romans 8 is a great example of the disparity and disunity in the Dominionist world. DeMar says fulfilled, Gentry says future. These (major) disagreements brings to light the irony and illogic of men such as Mathison who wrote: "The first thing that must be noted about full preterism is that it is not a monolithic movement. There are disagreements over the interpretation and application of key texts and concepts even among the advocates of full preterism" (*Postmillennialism*, 1999, 235). So, leading postmillennialists differ drastically on foundational eschatological prophecies. But that is fine, no problem! However, one should be cautious of the preterist movement because after all, there is some disagreement there! Ludicrous to say the least.

Romans 8 as predicting the future eschaton, takes a position on *kairos*, that virtually *demands* a first century fulfillment.

Commenting on Luke 12:56 McDurmon says this: "The phrase 'the present time' (*ton kairon de touton*, dkp) is an obvious eschatological/prophetic reference. To what particular 'time' did Jesus refer? ...Jesus refers to *this time*– that is, His and His audience's time– not some time of judgment in the future. Whatever he's talking about, it refers to the people he was talking to." (2011, 34*)*.

So, Jesus' referent to "the present time" i.e. *kairon touton*– "this time," demands that it referred to Jesus' time and his first century contemporary generation. This naturally raises an important question.

What was Paul's "the present time" in Romans 8? Was it different from Jesus' "this time" in Luke? It is to be noted that in Luke, Jesus did not use the stronger form used in Romans 8. Paul referred to "the now time" (*tou nun kairou*), in conjunction with the "about to be revealed" glory. Thus, the form of language emphasizes the contemporary nature of Paul's "the now time."

How then can McDurmon or anyone else, appeal to Luke and demand a first century fulfillment– based on an appeal to *kairos*– but then turn around and apply Romans, which even more powerfully emphasized the presence of the "now time" and extrapolate that text into the distant future? This is illogical and unwarranted.

Romans 8 undeniably anticipated the fulfillment of God's ultimate eschatological goal– the goal of Ephesians 1-- and Paul irrefutably posited the fulfillment of that goal as imminent. It was about to be revealed.

This is confirmed by a look at the term Paul uses in Ephesians 1, "the fulness of time."

**Paul said it was God's eternal purpose to reunite heaven and**

102

**earth in the fulness of time (Ephesians 1).**

**Paul said Christ appeared in the fulness of time (Galatians 4:4).**

**The fulness of time in which Christ appeared was the "end of the age" days of the Old Covenant (Hebrews 9:26), the last days (Hebrews 1:1). Christ appeared in the days of and under Torah.**

**Therefore, the "fulness of time" was the end of the age period of Torah– the last days of the Old Covenant age.**

Now, since Paul himself defines the fulness of time as the age of Torah– the last days of that age– then where is the justification for creating another "fulness of time" to insert into Ephesians 1?

Paul said the fulness of time was the last days of the Mosaic age. Peter, in Acts 3, said the prophets who foretold the restoration of all things spoke of "these days." We thus have an inescapable declaration that the time for the eschatological consummation was the first century. There is no way to make the reunification of heaven and earth and the restoration of all things typological of anything.

In Ephesians, Paul says the reunification was taking place. God was at work through and in Christ, to reunite and reconcile all things. In many ways, this is *the message* of Ephesians.

So, Paul said it was God's ultimate purpose to reunite all things in Christ, in the fulness of time. Paul said Christ appeared in the appointed fulness of times. He said God was reuniting all things in Christ. This is *prima facie* proof Paul was not talking about another reunification, another appointed fulness of times. It is, therefore, patently wrong to extrapolate to another climactic parousia. AD 70 was not a shadow of another, better, ultimate reunification. AD 70 was "the end of all things", the *completion* of the good work that had begun[116] (Philippians 1:6f).[117]

In anticipation of the next point, note that the reunification of "heaven and earth" is nothing less than the restoration of man to the Most Holy Place, the Presence of God.

Virtually all scholars agree that the Garden of Eden was the "Most Holy Place." Man was booted from that Presence due to sin, and "heaven and earth" were separated. It was God's eternal purpose to restore man to His Presence– both on earth, and in heaven. As we have just seen, Paul said the time appointed by God for that restoration / reunification was present. We are about to see that Hebrews says the restoration to the Most Holy Place– the "real" end-- is unequivocally placed at the end of the Old Covenant age– in AD 70.

---

[116] As mentioned earlier, there are several additional reasons for rejecting the idea that AD 70 was typological and Philippians 1 provides another of those strong reasons. Paul said Christ would perfect (*epitelesei*, second person, singular, future of *telos*). The addition of *epi* to *telos* gives us a "fully complete" meaning. So, Paul was predicting the complete fulfillment, the "finishing", if you will, of Christ's work, not a fulfillment pointing to another fulfillment.

[117] In my debate with McDurmon I noted from Colossians (which is parallel with Ephesians) how Paul utilizes the language of Genesis 1-3 to speak of the restoration work of Christ that was taking place even in his ministry. While McDurmon says there must be a physical restoration of material creation, Paul interpreted the Genesis restoration promises spiritually, fulfilled in Christ. He said not one word about physical dirt, or the postulated redemption of bugs, slugs and mosquitos. You would certainly think if God's ultimate purpose was the redemption of physical creation, he would not have completely omitted mentioning such in Ephesians and Colossians– which speak of God's ultimate goal.

104

---

**Reason #11 - Entrance into the Most Holy Place – the Restoration to the Presence of God - The Eschatological Goal - Was to Be at the End of the Old Covenant Age– Not the End of the Christian Age (Hebrews 9:6-10)**

---

"Now when these things had been thus prepared, the priests always went into the first part of the tabernacle, performing the services. But into the second part the high priest went alone once a year, not without blood, which he offered for himself and for the people's sins committed in ignorance; the Holy Spirit indicating this, that the way into the Holiest of All was not yet made manifest while the first tabernacle was still standing. It was symbolic for the present time in which both gifts and sacrifices are offered which cannot make him who performed the service perfect in regard to the conscience— concerned only with foods and drinks, various washings, and fleshly ordinances imposed until the time of reformation" (Hebrews 9:6-10).

In the Garden, man was in the presence of the Lord. It has long been recognized that the Garden was "the Most Holy Place."[118] It was where man met God in fellowship. In the Garden, in the Presence, man was truly "alive."

The entrance of sin led to man being kicked out of that Presence, out of the Most Holy Place.[119] When man was kicked out of the Garden,

---

[118] See for instance Beale, *The Temple and the Church's Mission*, (Downer's Grove, InterVarsity2004)26: "The Garden of Eden was the first archetypal temple."

[119] For an extended discussion of the Most Holy Place and its significance to eschatological and covenantal

*he died that very day.*[120] However, it was YHVH's (eternal) purpose to restore that Presence. Restoration to the Most Holy Place is nothing but *resurrection*. See our discussion above on Ephesians 1:10.

The Law of Moses was given to Israel to exacerbate the awareness of sin and alienation from the Lord (Romans 5:20-21) and thus, the need for reconciliation.

While Torah reminded man of his alienation, the Temple in the midst of Israel (cf. Ezekiel 5:8-9) was nonetheless the shining symbol of God's presence in their midst-- at least on one level. Yet, even that marvelous edifice symbolized the on-going separation– the dividing veil– between God and man: "The Spirit is indicating this, that the way into the MHP is not made manifest, while the first tabernacle is still standing. or still has standing" (Hebrews 9:8).

It is important to note Hebrews is not saying there was no access to the Lord's presence as long as the Tabernacle / Temple was physically standing. The meaning of the text is that as long as the temple praxis, with its "gifts and sacrifices ... foods and drinks, various washings, and fleshly ordinances" had abiding *validity* as God's divinely revealed system, there was no access.

---

studies, see my written debate with Kurt Simmons: *The End of Torah: At the Cross or AD 70?* The book is available from my websites, Kindle, Amazon and other retailers.

[120] The widespread misunderstanding and wrong definition of the death Adam died the very day he ate lies at the root of virtually all eschatological confusion. To wrongly identify the death of Adam is to wrongly identify the nature of the resurrection. The language of Genesis is clear and unambiguous "in the day you eat, you will surely die." God did not say they would *begin* to die and He did not say they would die *900 years later*! See my book, *We Shall Meet Him In The Air,* for an extended discussion of the death of Adam.

Ellingworth says, "Some scholars, including P. E. Hughes and Teodorico, give the meaning of "have status" or "legal standing" or "function."[121] The Word Commentary concurs: "The Holy Spirit disclosed to the writer that as long as the front compartment of the tabernacle had cultic status, access to the presence of God was not yet available to the congregation." "So long as the cultic ordinances of the Sinaitic covenant were a valid expression of God's redemptive purpose and the front compartment *exouses stasin*, "had cultic status', entrance into the MHP was not yet accessible. There can be access only after the front compartment has been set aside."[122]

Robertson comments on Hebrews 9: "Another genitive absolute with the present active participle of *echo* (having standing, *stasin*, 'the first tabernacle having a place."[123] Finally, "So long as the fore-tent has an appointed place as part of the Divine arrangements for worship."[124]

We could multiply this kind of quote, but this will suffice. The point is well established that as long as the Old Covenant Temple cultus had validity there was no access to the presence of God.

Robertson takes note of the powerful temporal force of the text, when the author says those sacrifices and the entire cultus was spoken of as "a parable for the present time" (9:9). He says the language indicates "For the present crisis' (kairon, not aiona, not chronon, time). Perfect

---

[121] Charles Ellingworth, New International Greek Testament Commentary, (Carlisle, Paternoster, 1993)437, 439.

[122] William Lane, *Word Biblical Commentary, Hebrews, 9-13, Vol. 47b*, (Dallas, Word, 1991)223.

[123] John A. T. Robertson's *Word Pictures In the New Testament*, Vol 5, (Nashville, Broadman, 1932)397.

[124] Robertson Nicoll, *Expositors Greek Testament*, Vol. 4, (Grand Rapids, Eerdmans, 1970)330.

active articular (repeated article) participle of enistemi (intransitive), the age in which they lived, not the past, not the future." (1932, Vol. V, 397). In other words, the author of Hebrews was impressing on his audience the typological import of the Old Covenant *was focused on their time*– the appointed time.

It is more than apparent therefore, that the Mosaic Cultus was an interim system intended to endure until the types and shadows of its sacrifices and washings, etc. found realization / fulfillment. In other words, as long as that system of worship continued to exist *as a system of types and shadows* there was no access to God. But, those types and shadows point to "the time of reformation" (v. 10) when access to the MHP would be opened to all.

According to most commentators, the time of reformation is the equivalent to the "restoration of all things" i.e. the eschatological consummation of Acts 3:23f. Ellingworth says that in Jewish thought *diorthosis* (i.e. reformation in Hebrews 9:10) referred to "the age to come," and he equates it to Acts 3 and *apokatastasis* (i.e. restoration).[125]

Robertson in his respective commentaries on Acts[126] and Hebrews, shows where *apokatastasis* (restoration -Acts 3) was used in medical texts to speak of setting health back aright. The word was used by some Jewish writers to speak of the New Heaven and Earth. Likewise, in his commentary on Hebrews, he says *diorthosis (Hebrews 9:10)* was used in medical texts in the identical way. In other words, for Robertson, *apokatastasis* and *diorthosis* are synonyms indicative of the eschatological climax.

---

[125] Paul Ellingworth, *New International Greek Testament Commentary, Hebrews*, (Carlisle, Paternoster, 1993)444.

[126] A. T. Robertson, *Word Pictures in the NT, Acts*, (Nashville, Broadman, 1930)46f.

Gentry, commenting on Acts 3 offers this: "The force of the 'until' (until the times of restoration, DKP) makes the times of restitution simultaneous with Christ's mediatorial session in heaven. He will come again not to introduce the restitution predicted by the prophets, but because He shall then have completed it." (Citing Wilmot). (2009, 501). He then adds: "The restoration is a reformation that supplants the old order (Hebrews 9:10). It is a process leading to 'the regeneration' of the fallen world as a system (John 1:29; 3:17;4:42), where Christ's will shall be done in the earth..... Christ will not return bodily until this reformation / restoration / regeneration process has overwhelmed the kingdom of Satan on earth. The battle between these rival kingdoms takes place on earth and in time." (2009, 502).

Take particular note how Gentry equates the consummation of the restoration with the time of reformation– *citing Hebrews 9:10!* This is a fatal connection for Gentry's Postmillennial futurism. Let me express it succinctly:

**The restoration of all things is the reformation that supplants the old order (Hebrews 9:10, Gentry).**

**Christ does not return until this reformation has overwhelmed the kingdom of Satan.[127]**

**But, the time of reformation is the end of the Old Covenant Order- (Hebrews 9:6-10).**

**Therefore, Christ does not return until the end of the Old**

---

[127] Interestingly, when commenting on Romans 16:20 which predicted the destruction of Satan, Gentry and many Dominionists see AD 70 as the fulfillment. McDurmon affirmed this in our debate. Well, is not the destruction of Satan, as posited in Romans 16, not the destruction of Satan at the end of the millennium? If not, why not?

## Covenant Order.

Patently, if the restoration of all things is the same as the time of reformation, as posited by most scholars[128] and if the time of reformation was to be at the fulfillment of the typological world of Israel in AD 70, then it is inescapably true that the eschatological climax occurred in AD 70. This is definitive, irrefutable proof that AD 70 was not a type or shadow of a still future consummation.

Clearly, access to the presence of the Lord would come at the end of that typological Old Covenant system. This is "covenant eschatology" in its purest form and illustrates the fallacy of modern Dispensationalism.

Premillennial author Pentecost claimed, "Eschatological studies are not concerned with...the Mosaic Covenant made by God with man, inasmuch as all these are temporary and non-determinative in respect to future things, but only with the four eternal covenants given by God, by which He has obligated Himself in relation to the prophetic program." (1980, 67).

In the light of Hebrews 9, nothing could be further from the truth. The "Second Coming " of Christ, to bring man into the MHP, would be at the *diorthosis*, the time of reformation. But, the time of reformation is undeniably at the end of Torah. Thus, nothing is more inseparably tied to eschatology than the Mosaic Covenant and its termination. Clearly, the Hebrews author posits the restoration of the Edenic fellowship with the Presence *at the end of the Mosaic age*. But this is not only true of Hebrews 9.

---

[128] See my *Like Father Like Son, On Clouds of Glory* for a much fuller discussion of the meaning of *apokatastasis* and *diorthosis* and the implications of the correlation between Acts 3 and Hebrews 9. That book is available on Amazon, my websites, Kindle and other retailers.

In Revelation we likewise have the concept of the entrance into the Most Holy Place and few would deny that Revelation is about the consummation of the eschatological drama.

In Revelation 15:8, John, after seeing the Ark of the Testimony in the heavenly temple (cf. Revelation 11:15) was told there would be no entrance into the Most Holy Place until the wrath of God, in the seventh vial, was completed in the judgment of Babylon.

Space forbids a full discussion of the identity of Babylon, but, there is a wide array of excellent documentation available and more comes available all the time, showing that Babylon of Revelation was none other than Old Covenant Jerusalem.[129] After all, it was, "where the Lord was slain" (Revelation 11:8). Notice what this means:

**There would be no entrance into the Most Holy Place while the typological Old Covenant system remained valid (Hebrews 9).**

**But, entrance into the Most Holy Place would be made available at the judgment of Babylon, i.e. Old Covenant Jerusalem (Revelation 15-16).[130]**

---

[129] See Kenneth Gentry's excellent tome, *Before Jerusalem Fell*, (Fountain Inn, SC., Victorious Hope Publishing, 2010). As well as my own *Who Is This Babylon?* (Ardmore, Ok. JaDon Management, 2011). For both historical and scriptural documentation. Both books are available from my websites.

[130] The constant vacillation of Keith Mathison is demonstrated in regard to the identity of Babylon of Revelation. In his *Postmillennialism* book, (1999, 153), Mathison identified Babylon as Jerusalem. But in his 2009 *Age To Age* book (689), he says Babylon was Rome. He seems not to realize that if this is true, man's entrance into the presence of God *was dependent on the fall of Rome*, hundreds of years after Revelation was written. Yet, he constantly emphasizes, at

**Therefore, the end of the typological Old Covenant system and entrance into the Most Holy Place would occur at the judgment of Babylon, i.e. Old Covenant Jerusalem.**

Now, the point of what we are saying is it was the Old Covenant age of types and shadows that "stood in the way" of the restoration of the Edenic fellowship with the Presence. It was not the Christian age.

Contra Bahnsen who spoke of the Old Covenant Sabbath foreshadowing the ultimate Sabbath, but then being replaced with a Christian Sabbath that now foreshadows the true rest, Hebrews sees no such schema. *There was but one interim system of types and shadows* and when it passed, the true Sabbath[131] rest in the presence of God would be (*was*) realized.[132]

---

least when debating millennialists, the imminence of the fulfillment of Revelation. We have the right to ponder what the fall of Rome had to do with man's entrance into the Presence of God. In scripture, it was the Old Covenant world that stood as the barrier between man and God (Hebrews 9:6-10).

[131] The issue of the typological Sabbath is incredibly important to the entire study of eschatology– and problematic for the futurist views. The Sabbath, per all scholars, foreshadowed the final salvation and resurrection. In my debate with McDurmon, I raised this issue several times, noting that Jesus said not a single iota of Torah– which included the seventh day Sabbath, as well as the festal, ceremonial Sabbaths– would pass until what they foreshadowed, i.e. final salvation, was fully realized. McDurmon admitted that he believes a lot of the jots and tittles of the Sabbath observance have passed and yet, what they foreshadowed remains unfulfilled. He refused to actually engage with the problems this presents to his eschatology.

[132] Seriah castigates true preterists for saying entrance into the MHP did not take place until AD 70. He is adamant that, "John (in Revelation, DKP) sees uncountable

Hebrews and Revelation undeniably posit the restoration of that lost fellowship at the time of the fulfillment of the types and shadows of the Old Covenant age-- not at the end of any proposed types and shadows of the New Covenant age.[133]

If the Edenic fellowship was restored at the end of the Old Covenant age, then what better restoration, what better "Sabbath rest," could be foreshadowed by the New Covenant system? Hebrews 9:6-10 definitively falsifies the idea that the end of Torah foreshadows the end of the New Covenant age. It posits restoration to the Presence, thus, the resurrection to "life" at the end of Torah. There is no greater eschatology than this. If man has been restored to the Presence,[134] the

---

numbers of saints in heaven, before AD 70, with Christ." And yet, Seriah does not believe the Old Covenant heaven and earth– i.e. Torah, passed until AD 70, which is where Hebrews 9 posits entrance into the MHP. Likewise, Seriah identifies Babylon as Old Covenant Jerusalem, but, he either overlooks or ignores the fact that John emphatically states there was no entrance into the MHP until the wrath of God was finished– in the judgment of Babylon. To say Seriah has "missed the point" therefore, is an understatement.

[133] It is fascinating and, perhaps significant, to see how the Dominionist literature virtually ignores Hebrews 9:6-10 and Revelation 15:8. The entire issue of entrance into the MHP is all but ignored. These passages are seldom even mentioned in the works of the men we have been citing in this work.

[134] There is a huge disparity in evangelical Christianity. It is commonly believed that when the Christian dies today, they go directly to heaven, which of course, is the MHP! Yet, we are told, being in the Presence is not enough. We must one day leave heaven– the Christian hope– and come back to earth, to get a resuscitated, restored body, *which we had not needed to be in heaven*, and then go back to heaven where we had been already!

resurrection, in fulfillment of Genesis 2-3 has been fulfilled.

Entrance into the Most Holy Place would be the restoration of the Edenic fellowship with God.
It is nothing other than the resurrection.
Hebrews posits the restoration of that fellowship *at the end of the Torah.*
If, therefore, the Edenic fellowship (life) was restored at the end of Torah in AD 70, then what more could AD 70 point to typologically?
The restoration of what was lost in Eden is the climax of the story of eschatology!

> **Reason #12 - The First Century Church Had Arrived at Zion– The Locus of the Eschatological, End of the Millennium, Resurrection.**

"But you have come to Mount Zion and to the city of the living God, the heavenly Jerusalem, to an innumerable company of angels, 23 to the general assembly and church of the firstborn who are registered in heaven, to God the Judge of all, to the spirits of just men made perfect" (Hebrews 12:21-23).

In Messianic prophecy, *nothing* is more central than Zion. In Isaiah alone there are 45 references to the kingdom capital and at least 30 of them are patently Messianic / eschatological. We can only address a few of the Zion prophecies here. Our purpose is to briefly demonstrate that Zion was the prophetic locus of the eschatological consummation.

The Temple was considered the theological center of the earth (Ezekiel 5:8-9). To gain some idea of the significance of Zion/Jerusalem one can scan the Psalms and read there the descriptions. In Psalms 50:2 the writer calls the city "the perfection of beauty." Read the book of Lamentations as Jeremiah considered the once magnificent city now in ruins after the Babylonian invasion.

The *Encyclopedia Judaica* says, "The Temple and its appurtenances were pictured as symbolizing the entire universe, including the stars of the firmament and the Temple service was considered to be a source of blessing to all the nations of the world and even to the heavens and the earth and all it contains.[135] In many ways, the temple was considered to be "heaven and earth."[136]

Every male Jew had to travel to Jerusalem every year to observe the feast days (Leviticus 23). Copies of the Law were kept at Jerusalem and there the great Rabbis expounded the Law. It was only in Jerusalem that acceptable worship could be offered to the Lord (Deuteronomy 12/ John 4).

Legally, the decisions of the Sanhedrin at Jerusalem were considered paramount even though other cities had minor Sanhedrins to handle local issues. Thus, from almost any perspective Zion was truly the center of the world for the Jews. But Zion was also the center of the world from a prophetic perspective.

It is both interesting and sad that in the Amillennial tradition- My former belief-- one aspect of some of these predictions is emphasized while other equally significant subjects are totally ignored or divorced from the elements being emphasized. For instance, in Isaiah 2-4 the prophet predicted the establishment of the house of the Lord on the Mountain of the Lord, i.e. Zion.

What is often ignored, or even denied, is the *judgment* context of that establishment (Isaiah 2:4, the Day of the Lord (2:10f),[137] the time of

---

[135] Encyclopedia Judaiaca, Vol. 15, p. 984.

[136] See my *The Elements Shall Melt With Fervent Heat,* where I demonstrate from Josephus, the OT and other sources that the Jews considered the temple to be "heaven and earth." The book is available from my websites, on Kindle, Amazon and other retailers.

[137] In Luke 23:28-31 Jesus quotes from Isaiah 2:11-21 in his prediction of the fall of Jerusalem. Paul, in 2 Thessalonians 1:9-10 quotes the identical verses as did Jesus. Now since Jesus applied Isaiah 2 to the fall of Jerusalem, what

Israel's judgment (3:10-24), the time when the Branch of the Lord would be glorified at his coming (4:2), the salvation of the remnant in that day (4:3) and the establishment of the new tabernacle of God (4:6). All of these are constituent elements of Isaiah's "last days" prediction.

Yet the Amillennialist historically gives little attention to these subjects outside of Isaiah 2:2-3. If attention is given to these items, "gap-ology"[138] takes over and huge gaps of time are injected between the establishment of the church, supposedly complete on Pentecost and the judgment of verses 4f, 9f; 19-21. Or, 2:2-3 is applied to Pentecost, but the "end of time" is inserted into 2:10f.

The Amillennialist therefore, makes the prediction of Isaiah 2-4 a panoramic view of history, with occasional "flashbacks" for those items that cannot be extended into the future, extending over the millennia.[139] This finds no support in the context.

---

right does the modern commentator have to apply 2 Thessalonians, which springs from Isaiah, to an "end of time"?

[138] Both the amillennialists and postmillennialists castigate the Dispensationalist for their "gap theory" i.e. inserting temporal gaps into "troublesome" scriptures. And yet, both of these other schools are just as guilty of inserting gaps into the Biblical record as are the dispensationalists! I will not discuss this here, but will be writing on it in the near future.

[139] The same is true of the postmillennialists. Gentry identifies the last days of Isaiah 2 as the Christian age (2009, 206f). However, he does not even mention Isaiah 2:10, 19-21 and the Day of the Lord *that would bring the last days to an end.* However, Gentry applies Luke 23:28-31 to the AD 70 fall of Jerusalem. The significance of this is that in Luke, Jesus is directly citing Isaiah 2 and the prediction of the Day of the Lord! In another example of Postmillennial confusion,

The point here is that in Isaiah 2-4 Zion is the locus of the kingdom. From there "the Word of the Lord" i.e. the New Covenant, would go forth to all the nations.

Isaiah 24-27 likewise contains a highly important "Zion" prophecy. And for our purpose in this work, it may well be the most significant of the Zion prophecies.

In Isaiah 24 we find the destruction of "heaven and earth" as a result of Israel's violation of Torah. Even McDurmon acknowledges this judgment is not the end of the world, but rather the judgment on Israel for violation of the Law of Moses: "The ESV notes rightly that the word "earth" could as well be translated "land" as throughout the passage. This is more likely, since the passage clearly applies to a people who broke the everlasting covenant, and these could only be Israel at that time. So, the Hebrew word *eretz* here refers to the land of Israel, not the whole 'earth' in the modern sense. And note the clearly covenantal punishment: the kingdom would be left desolate (Exodus 23:29; Leviticus 26:33f; Luke 11:17) and the people few." (2011, 59).

McDurmon's problem here is limiting the prophecy to Isaiah's day. Very clearly, the NT writers draw on the Little Apocalypse for their eschatology, including the millennium and the rule of YHVH on Zion (24:21f).

The prophecy continues into chapter 25 where the Lord promised to create the Messianic Banquet "on this mountain" i.e. Zion, in the day He would swallow up death forever (v. 6-8).

The Messianic nature of the prophecy continues into chapter 26:19f a prophecy of the resurrection in the Day the Lord . He would come

---

McDurmon applies Isaiah 2:2-4 to the span of history, (2011, 15) while on the other hand affirming the "last days" is referent to Israel's last days (2011, 47+).

out of the heavens to avenge the blood of the martyrs. In chapter 27:1f this Day would be when Leviathan, the Serpent, would be destroyed. At that time the Lord would forsake the people He had created, destroy the fortified city and turn the altar into chalkstones.

So, very clearly, this is a Messianic prophecy of the last days, the establishment of the kingdom at the end of the millennium resurrection.

Note how Isaiah 25:8 is one of the sources for Paul's doctrine and his hope of the "final" resurrection, the resurrection at the end of the millennium.

In other words, Isaiah was predicting, not some typological resurrection, not some Day of the Lord pointing to another Day of the Lord. He was predicting the realization of the "restoration of all things." He was prophesying the reconciliation of "heaven and earth" when man would once again be restored to the Edenic Presence- the Most Holy Place.

Let me put this as succinctly as possible:

**Paul's doctrine of the resurrection– the "final" resurrection that would occur at the end of the millennium- was taken from, and based on Isaiah 25:8 (1 Corinthians 15:55-56).**

**The resurrection of Isaiah 25:8 would be centered in "Zion."**

**Therefore, the "final" resurrection that would occur at the end of the millennium would be centered in Zion.**

Note also the Messianic Banquet of v. 6 would be "on this mountain" i.e. Zion. So, the Messianic Banquet and the end of the millennium resurrection are located "on this mountain" God's holy hill Zion.

A quick observation here about Zion that further illustrates the inconsistency of the Dominionist hermeneutic. In my debate with McDurmon, I argued extensively about the importance of Zion. I noted McDurmon himself says that in scripture "Zion" has been "spiritualized....and fulfilled in the body of Christ" (2011, 178). He likewise claims Abraham, Isaac and Jacob have sat down at the Messianic kingdom banquet (2011, 64).

I noted that if Abraham and the worthies sat down at the Banquet then of necessity, the final resurrection has been fulfilled. McDurmon's answer was he did not find the word "final" or "last resurrection" in Isaiah, therefore, it cannot be proven that Isaiah predicted the end of the millennium resurrection.

I responded with the following chart:[140]

---

[140] The McDurmon -V- Preston Debate is available from my websites, Amazon, Kindle and other retailers.

Joel Distinguishes Between Texts Because of the Use of Different Words, or the Omission of Words, i.e. "Final Is Not There!"

Consider the Following, However...

Acts 1 Does Not Mention the "Final" Time of the End, The Trumpet, the resurrection, or use the word "parousia" – Like 1 Cor. 15 does

1 Corinthians 15 does not mention the 1000 yrs, "final end", coming with the angels, opening of the books, the Book of Life of Rev. 20

1 Thessalonians 4 says not one word about the millennium, the passing of earth and heaven of Revelation 20- the "final end!"

Revelation 20:10-12 Does Not Mention the parousia with the angels, the trumpet, the shout, the "final" end of time!

Yet, Joel says these texts are the same

Different Elements– Or Omission of Elements / Words– Does Not Demand "Different times or Topics in Apocalyptic literature!

Incredibly, Joel *said* he agreed with my chart and my claim that you cannot "screw down apocalyptic language" so tightly that the absence of given words, or the use of different words, demands different topics or times are in view. But, notice what happened then.

When I pressed my points on Isaiah 24-27, the Banquet and the resurrection, Joel *repeated his claim* that the absence of the word "final," or "last" means Isaiah does not necessarily predict the "final" resurrection!

I noted that in 1 Corinthians 7, Paul dealt with those who were evidently pondering whether, since the New Creation had broken into the Old, they should still be married. Paul told them to stay married. This is a powerful refutation of McDurmon's argument on "no

121

marrying" in the New Creation. Joel's response? Well, he said because the words "New Creation" are not found in 1 Corinthians 7, my argument fails!

Joel re-adopted his "last hermeneutic", the very hermeneutic he said was false! He said the absence of words refuted my argument. When I demonstrated the fallacy of that hermeneutic he said he agreed that the absence of words does not demand difference of topics. But then, cornered, he once again said the absence of words demands different topics! His desperation was obvious to everyone.

Other Dominionists, including McDurmon's employer, DeMar, *ostensibly at least*, rejects McDurmon's hermeneutic.

DeMar wrote in response to Dispensational writers who argued that missing words, text to text, demands different topics and different times! For instance, the word "church" is not found in Revelation 4-22, therefore, Revelation cannot be discussing the church. Sound familiar?

DeMar responded, citing Gundry: "Unless we are prepared to relegate large chunks of the NT to limbo of irrelevance to the Church, we cannot make the mention or omission of the term 'church' a criterion for determining the applicability of a passage to saints of the present age.'" DeMar then adds: "Is the Bible interpretation based on word counts? The same reasoning process has been taken with the book of Esther: There can be no doubt that the historicity and canonicity of Esther has been the most debated of all the OT books. Even some Jewish scholars questioned the inclusion in the OT because of the absence of God's name.' If word counts are to be so heavily relied upon then Lindsey refutes himself. He finds the Antichrist all over the book of Revelation, but the word is nowhere to be found." (*Madness*, 1994, 184).

While it *appears* as if DeMar rejects the dispensational hermeneutic–and McDurmon's-- *later in the same work* he wrote–

"For those who claim that it is (the gathering, *episunagogee*, being the rapture, DKP) we must ask why Paul would use a different word in his second letter to clear up a supposed misunderstanding about what the Thessalonians thought he meant concerning 'our being *caught up* to him' in his first letter. Why didn't Paul write, 'With regard to our being caught up to Him? The answer is quite obvious: Paul is discussing two separate events." (1994, 318).

So, DeMar castigates the dispensational hermeneutic of positing two comings of Christ because of missing words, or the use of different words in separate texts. Then, because 2 Thessalonians 2 uses a different word (i.e. one word is missing in one text that is present in another) from 1 Thessalonians 4, this demands that Paul was discussing two different comings, of radically different nature from each other, at two different times. To say this is inconsistent and self-contradictory is a huge understatement.

So, McDurmon contradicted himself, and, he contradicted his own employer – who contradicted *himself*– when he argued that missing words demand different topics, subjects or times.[141] Confusing to say the least.

But, let's take a look at the Dominionist views of Zion, because, to say the least, the prevailing views are self-destructive of a futurist eschatology.

---

[141] Gentry accepts McDurmon's hermeneutic on missing words or different words demanding different topics, subjects or times, however. He claims, for instance, that because 2 Thessalonians 1 uses a different word for coming (*elthe*, from *erchomai*) from 2 Thessalonians 2:1-3 (*parousia*) that two different comings are in view. Gentry's self contradictions on this are fatal, as I demonstrate in my *We Shall Meet Him In The Air, the Wedding of the King of kings*. I offer there an extensive expose of Gentry's (and by extension, McDurmon's) hermeneutic.

123

DeMar, when writing against the Dispensational emphasis on Old Covenant Israel, says all promises to Old Covenant Israel have been fulfilled.[142] Well, Isaiah 24-27– and the promise of the resurrection, was an Old Covenant promise, made to Old Covenant Israel.

Mathison is on record affirming the fulfillment of God's Zion promises. Commenting on Hebrews 11-12, Mathison says of chapter 12: "Christians are now experiencing the fulfillment of the eschatological hopes of Israel." (2009, 625).

In another work, commenting on the same texts in Hebrews, he says: "Under the New Covenant we *have come* to Mt. Zion. We *have come* to the heavenly Jerusalem. We *have come* to the church of the firstborn. We *have come* to Jesus, the mediator of this glorious New Covenant.... That which the Old Testament believers looked for in faith has come, and they have now received what was promised"[143]

To say Mathison's views are problematic is to understate the case:
1.) If Christians are currently enjoying the fulfillment of Israel's eschatological hope and promises, then the resurrection– which was the hope of Israel– has been fulfilled.
2.) If the OT worthies have now received what was promised, then, again, the end of the millennium resurrection has been fulfilled.
3.) If the OT worthies have received what was promised them, then the NT saints have received it, because Paul taught that the OT and NT saints would receive the promises at the same time (Hebrews 11:39f).

McDurmon, also arguing against the Dispensationalists, argues

---

[142] Dated October 14, 2005:

http://americanvision.org/1728/all-promises-made-israel-have-been-fulfilled-answering-replacement-theology-critics-part-4/

[143] Keith Mathison, *Postmillennialism: An Eschatology of Hope*, (Philippsburg, NJ, 1999)135. (His emphasis).

effectively for the fulfillment of the Zion promises:

> "When the argument of faith and pilgrimage in Hebrews 11 finally does turn to "us" it notes a complete change of status. While all of those Old Testament pilgrims died and "did not receive what was promised," New Testament believers are different: "God had provided something better for *us*" (Heb. 11:40). So, we are categorically *not* like them. We are in a better position than they. The promised Kingdom has indeed come, it is given to us. We are not exiles waiting to receive the promise. Indeed, the author tells the first-century believing Jews in the very next chapter, as a continuation of the argument in Hebrews 11, "you have come to Mount Zion" (Heb. 12:22). They were no longer exiles; they had arrived!
>
> This arrival verse is very important. Horton refers to the Christians as pilgrims. He denies we have arrived, or downplays it in any meaningful sense. He constantly refers to Zion as a future destination: the "path to Zion," "this journey to Zion," "Marching to Zion." But Hebrews makes it absolutely clear that New Testament believers "have come to Zion." This is in the past tense. Horton says nothing about this verse, and yet it is the culmination of the argument the author began in Hebrews 11."[144]

In his book, *Jesus V Jerusalem*, McDurmon says the prophecies concerning Zion have been "spiritualized...and fulfilled in the body of Christ." (2011, 178).

The reader simply *must* catch the power of these admissions and

---

[144] http://americanvision.org/4445/the-great-omission/

affirmations from the Dominionist camp. On the one hand they tell us the prophecies concerning Zion have been fulfilled. God's Old Covenant promises made to Israel have *all* been fulfilled. On the other hand, they tell us we are waiting for the fulfillment of God's Old Testament promise (to Israel) of the resurrection– *centered in Zion*– to occur at the end of the Christian age. They tell us the spiritual fulfillment of those Zion resurrection promises must foreshadow another (real) resurrection at the end of another age. To say the least, this is specious. and it brings up a huge problem for instance, for McDurmon.

A brief sidebar: We have noted that in my debate with McDurmon, he claimed the physical types of the Old Covenant foreshadowed the spiritual realities of Christ which have been fulfilled. However, the spiritual things of Christ are now the shadows of future things which are literal and physical,[145] i.e. Abraham, while he has now sat down at the kingdom table, as promised in Isaiah 25:6-8--> Matthew 8:11, is still looking for the true, the real promised land and city, which is literal and physical.

But, go back to McDurmon's arguments against the Dispensationalist immediately above. McDurmon argues convincingly that the promises of Zion are spiritualized and fulfilled and the dispensational anticipation of a future earthly restoration of Zion– and thus, logically of the land promises– are false.

Yet, McDurmon's debate argument leads directly to the dispensational paradigm! He says one of these days Abraham will be resurrected from the dirt and given the earth to rule, ostensibly from (literal) Zion. This is precisely what the Dispensationalists believe!

---

[145] As we have shown, Bahnsen likewise said the OT Sabbath foreshadowed the NT Sabbath which now foreshadows the real end.

What is the difference between the Dominionist arguing that *eventually*, Abraham is physically resurrected and rules physically on the earth and the Dispensationalist who argues that one day Abraham will be physically raised and possess the physical dirt in the kingdom?

Interestingly, both schools posit a long temporal gap between promise and fulfillment. God set the time for the fulfillment of the Abrahamic land promises, i.e. after "the fourth generation" of being in Egypt (Genesis 15:16f). However, according to McDurmon, Abraham did not receive the promise at the appointed time, although his descendants did.[146] Likewise, the dispensationalists say Abraham never received the land promises and there has been so far a 4000 year gap between promise and fulfillment. But back to the point.

Paul was not anticipating a typological resurrection in 1 Corinthians 15, 1 Thessalonians 4, etc.. If so, where is the evidence of this? Revelation 20 did not predict a "kind of resurrection" pointing to another "real" resurrection.

But as I noted, in my debate with McDurmon he said there was in fact "a fulfillment" of 1 Corinthians 15 and Revelation 20.

Among other things, I challenged McDurmon to document from the church fathers or the creeds where this was anything even remotely resembling "orthodoxy." (See my earlier demonstration of how the Dominionists directly contradict the creeds). Of course, he made no attempt to produce such evidence, for that evidence does not exist. This is a brand new doctrine, newly invented virtually in our day,

---

[146] During the debate I noted repeatedly that in scripture Abraham received the land *through* his descendants (cf. Deuteronomy 34:1-4). This is representative fulfillment. For instance, Abraham was to rule the world *through his seed*. Christ is his seed, who has all authority. I offered other examples of this, but McDurmon ignored all of these arguments and facts.

mostly by the Reformed, partial preterist camp.

The irony here should not be lost. The Dominionists, especially Gentry, Mathison and others, constantly condemn the true preterist view because it is not creedal or cannot be found in the early church writings.[147] Although he did not make a major issue of it in our debate, McDurmon did appeal to the fact that Covenant Eschatology is not in the creeds, and that this should be considered.

The next point of contention is, where is the contextual indication that Paul looked beyond that admitted AD 70 fulfillment to another, true one? What is the *exegetical support* for this claim? Where does John even give so much as a syllable of support?

The truth is there is no textual, contextual, hermeneutical support for the Dominionist claims that AD 70 was typological. Their admissions that the Zion prophecies have been "spiritualized" and "fulfilled in the body of Christ" are fatal to their paradigm.

Notice what the Hebrews author says of the Zion promises: "You have come to Mt. Zion."[148]

---

[147] See my *The Elements Shall Melt With Fervent Heat* (233ff) for a revealing discussion of the self contradictions in the Postmillennial world in regard to the creeds. On the one hand they condemn Covenant Eschatology because it is non-creedal. Yet, increasingly, they are making theological arguments not found anywhere in the creeds or the fathers. Gentry acknowledges that his identification of Babylon in Revelation is not creedal, but says the evidence should be considered on its own merit. Well, *Amen!* Why should not the entire study of eschatology be decided on its own merit, based on *Sola Scriptura* and not the creeds or the fathers?

[148] We will not develop it here, but, Zion is also tied directly to salvation (Isaiah 46:13), the parousia (Isaiah

To the Hebrew mind *nothing* could more powerfully express the genuine, objective nearness of the resurrection, the restoration of all things! Zion was, as we have noted, the locus of every soteriological and eschatological tenet found in prophecy. The kingdom, salvation, the New Covenant, the Presence of the Lord, the Wedding, the resurrection, *everything*!

It would have been impossible for the Hebraic mind to believe Hebrews 12 meant: "You have come to the time when God is going to establish another typological Zion. He is going to sorta, kinda fulfill the resurrection, but only as a shadow of the real thing. So, you have come to the initial fulfillment of the Zion prophecies. But the real fulfillment will not be for who knows how long!" Such an idea is not to be found in the inspired text and should not be entertained by Bible students.

---

In Messianic prophecy, Zion was the ultimate goal. It is the capital of the kingdom, the source of the New Covenant, the Messianic Wedding Banquet and the resurrection.

For the Hebrews author to declare: "You have come to Mount Zion" was nothing but a profound and thrilling declaration that the goal of their eschatological expectation had arrived!

He was not saying another time of waiting for types and shadows to be fulfilled had come!

Truly, the end of all things had drawn near!

---

59:16ff), and the New Creation (Isaiah 65-66). It is therefore easy to see the "climactic" and consummative nature of the Hebrews' affirmation.

To put the argument simply:

The Old Testament prophecies concerning Zion, including the Messianic Banquet and the resurrection of the dead, were prophecies of the consummative eschatological resurrection.

But, the OT prophecies concerning Zion, including the resurrection of the dead, have been "spiritualized" and "fulfilled in the body of Christ" (Gentry, Mathison, McDurmon)

Therefore, the consummative, eschatological Messianic Banquet and the resurrection of the dead have been fulfilled.

Furthermore,

The Old Testament prophecies of the Messianic Banquet and the resurrection of the dead, prophecies of the consummative, "final" resurrection , were to be fulfilled "in Zion."

But, the first century saints had arrived at Zion (Hebrews 12:21f).

Therefore, the first century saints had arrived at the time for the fulfillment of the Messianic Banquet and the resurrection of the dead, the consummative, "final" resurrection.

Let me now tie together some of the previous points:
Peter said the time foretold for the restoration of all things was his first century "these days."
Paul said the goal of all previous ages had arrived.
He said "the end," the time of the final resurrection, would be at the end of Torah, the law that was the strength of sin.
Paul said the fulness of times, the time foreordained by God to reunite heaven and earth, was the last days of the Old Covenant age.
In Hebrews 9, the author says the entrance into the Most Holy Place, which is the restoration of Adamic fellowship, the reuniting of heaven and earth, the goal of all the ages, would be accomplished when

Israel's typological cultus was fulfilled and Torah no longer had validity.

And now, in Hebrews 12, the divine author told his audience they had arrived at the locus of the eschatological and Messianic expectation: "You have come to Mount Zion."

Each of these points, and especially when all are combined, tell the same tale. The eschatological consummation was to be at the end of the Old Covenant age of Israel. They have nothing to do with the end of time, or the end of the Christian age. That climax, at the end of Torah, was not prophetic of another consummation. The declaration is a definitive, irrefutable, incontrovertible refutation of the idea that AD 70 was a typological foreshadowing of the final fulfillment of the Zion promises.

# Why AD 70 Was Not A Type of Another End of The Age

---

**Reason #13 - The Judgment of the Living and the Dead Occurred in AD 70 - The Kingdoms of the World Became the Kingdom of God and His Christ**

---

Historically and creedally, the time of the judgment of the living and the dead is at the climactic, final end. Thus, if the judgment of the living and the dead occurred in AD 70 we can give no credence to the claim that AD 70 was typlogical of another, yet future, judgment of the living and the dead.

In his *Postmillennialism, An Eschatology of Hope* work Mathison documents (1999,244ff) the historical view of the church in regard to the judgment of the living and the dead. He does this to show how "unorthodox" the true preterist paradigm is. He says, "All branches of the visible church– Catholic, Orthodox and Protestant– have always understood the scriptures to teach that Christ is presently seated at the right hand of God and that He will return to judge the living and the dead" (1999, 244).

Mathison documents from church history, from the late second century forward, how church leaders, councils, creeds and commentators have taught , "He will come again with glory to judge the living and the dead." (Nicene Creed).

While this sounds like Mathison and the postmillennialists are in perfect alignment with all of that historical "orthodoxy" this simply is not true. What Mathison and other Dominionists do not reveal to their audiences is they are themselves clearly at direct and serious odds with the creeds and history themselves. See my discussion above.

For brevity, I will only give a short list of prophecies of "the judgment of the living and the dead." I will then demonstrate how postmillennialists claim those prophecies were fulfilled in AD 70, thus, setting themselves at a distance from the Creeds.

✦**Matthew 16:27-28** – "The Son of Man shall come, in the glory of the Father with his angels, and shall reward every man according to his works."
This is very clearly a comprehensive judgment, i.e. "Every man."

While the creeds assign Matthew 16:27 to the "end of time" *the Dominionists disagree.*

DeMar (1994, 34-35), Gentry (2010, 14), Leithart (2004, 42), Mathison (1999, 227+), Seriah (1999, 14), all affirm the AD 70 fulfilment of Matthew 16:27-28.

✦**Matthew 23:29-37**– "Upon you may come all the righteous blood, of all the righteous, from Abel unto Zecharias, whom you killed between the Temple and the altar."

Here is a comprehensive judgment– the vindication of all the martyrs. The judgment would encompass the dead as well as the living; thus, the judgment of the living and the dead.

Virtually all Dominionists posit fulfillment of Matthew 23 at AD 70.

✦ **Acts 17:30-31**; **Acts 24:14; 2 Timothy 4:1** - "There is about to be the resurrection of the just and unjust."

Paul uses the word "*mello*" to indicate the imminence of the judgment of the world. The lexicons are clear that a primary definition of this word, especially when used in the infinitive, is "about to be, to be on the point of."[149] It is interesting to see the vacillation of the

---

[149] See for instance Robinson and House, *Analytical Lexicon of New Testament Greek*, (Peabody, Mass.,

Dominionists in regard to *mello*.

Commenting on Romans 8 and the glory "to be revealed", DeMar appeals to *mello* to prove the first century fulfillment of Romans 8. (1994, 191). Mathison rejects the Dispensational view of Revelation 2-3 based on the fact John was told those things were "about to take place" (1999, 262– n 15). Gentry once appealed to *mello*, to establish the first century fulfillment of Revelation (1989, 141-142). However, when true preterists began pointing out Paul's use of *mello* in Acts to speak of the resurrection and judgment, Gentry quickly changed his views, although, he gave no convincing reasons for his change.

We have a perfect right to challenge the inconsistency of the postmillennialists in regard to *mello*. On the one hand, they see no problem affirming it means "about to be, on the point of." Yet, when the natural implications of this definition are noted, they suddenly equivocate and change directions. They do not do so due to linguistic, lexical evidence. No, they do so because of the preconceived, circular reasoning. Their argument, if such it may be called, is this: The judgment of the living and the dead is the resurrection. The resurrection is the raising of corpses out of the ground. That resurrection has not taken place, therefore, the use of *mello* in resurrection / judgment texts cannot mean "about to be." Sorry, but this is less than proper and less than convincing.

◆1 Peter 4:5-17 - V. 5– Christ was "ready" to judge the living and the dead." In v. 7, "the end of all things has drawn near." In v. 17, Peter said "the appointed time for the judgment has come."

---

Hendrickson, 2012)231. "With the infinitive, 'I am about to.'" Likewise, the Blass-DeBrunner Grammar says: "mellein with the infinitive expresses imminence." *Blass-DeBrunner, A Greek Grammar of the New Testament and Other Early Christian Literature*, (Chicago, University of Chicago Press, 1961)181.

Peter is clearly the source of much of the church's creedal theology of Jesus coming to judge the living and the dead. So, historically, the church has applied 1 Peter 4:5 to the final judgment.

Dominionists, at least some of them, strongly differ with the creeds on that application. Leithart applies this text to AD 70 (2004, 12-13). Seriah applies v. 5, to a yet future judgment, (1999, 82f) but applies v. 7 to AD 70 (1999, 14). This clearly overlooks and rejects the unity of Peter's discussion. It likewise ignores the use of the anaphoric article in v. 17. see just below.

Gentry also applies v. 7 to AD 70 (1994, 22, n. 36) but ignores v. 5 and v. 17. This is somewhat ironic in light of DeMar's hermeneutical exhortation: "One of the first things a Christian must learn in interpreting the Bible is to pay attention to the time texts" (1994, 27). Yet, DeMar ignores the time statements of v. 5 and v. 17 while emphasizing v. 7!

In my debate with McDurmon, I responded to his claims about Job and a physical resurrection, by appealing to 1 Peter.

Peter said Christ was "ready (Greek, *hetoimos*, meaning not only morally prepared, but *temporally ready)* to judge "the living and the dead" (1 Peter 4:5). He said, "the end of all things has drawn near" (v. 7). He said, "*the* time has come for *the* judgment to begin" (v. 17).

In verse 17 Peter used the *anaphoric article*, the preponderant use of the article in the Greek. What this means is a writer introduces a subject. In his later discussion of that subject, he uses the definite article to refer back to that subject. This means verse 17 refers back to v. 5. Thus, in verse 17, Peter said, "the time has come for the judgment of the living and the dead" i.e. the judgment of v. 5, the resurrection at "the end of all things"!

Peter affirmed the end of "all things." His declaration that the (divinely appointed) time had come for the judgment of the living and the dead undeniably refers to the resurrection of the dead– and demands a first century fulfillment. McDurmon never offered one word of response to my arguments on 1 Peter.

> Through inspiration, Peter said the divinely appointed time for "the judgment of the living and the dead" had arrived.
> Historical orthodoxy and the creeds simply deny or ignore Peter's words.
> Nothing could more directly challenge the blind allegiance to "church history", "historical orthodoxy", or the creeds.
> The choice is clear: Accept Peter's inspired words, or hold tenaciously to man made orthodoxy.

So, 1 Peter 4, in spite of the "historical and creedal view of the church" undeniably posited the judgment of the living and the dead in the first century. Historical "orthodoxy" and the creeds count nothing in the face of Peter's testimony. If (since) history and the creeds conflict with the inspired word it is time to set aside the creeds and historical orthodoxy and take *Sola Scriptura* seriously. The judgment of the living and the dead occurred in the first century.

✦**Revelation 11:15f** - "Then the seventh angel sounded: And there were loud voices in heaven, saying, "The kingdoms of this world have become the kingdoms of our Lord and of His Christ, and He shall reign forever and ever!" And the twenty-four elders who sat before God on their thrones fell on their faces and worshiped God, saying: "We give You thanks, O Lord God Almighty, The One who is and who was and who is to come, Because You have taken Your great power and reigned. The nations were angry, and Your wrath has come, And the time of the dead, that they should be judged, And that You should reward Your servants the prophets and the saints, And those who fear Your name, small and great, And should destroy those who destroy the earth."

In Dominionist circles, it is *very* common to see Revelation 11 applied to AD 70.

DeMar applies Revelation 11:15f to AD 70 ( 1994,173, 264, 288, 290). Gentry says the sounding of the seventh trumpet signaled the end of the Old Covenant world in AD 70 (2009, 407). Mathison sees Revelation 11 as fulfilled in the fall of Jerusalem and the overthrow of the Old Covenant age (1999)151f).[150]

McDurmon says: "God's answer to the prayer of the martyrs (Luke 18) would be "the great judgment He had just described in Luke 17:26-37; (see also Revelation 11:18)" (2011, 114).

Before his abandonment of the true preterist paradigm, Sam Frost wrote an outstanding piece in which he commented on Revelation 11. I give here an extended quote from that article.

"Further, they exclaim, "The nations were angry, and your wrath has come. The time for judging the dead and rewarding your servants the prophets and your saints" (11:18). Now, we have seen that 22:12 is entirely something John saw as "near," and Gentry concurs. We have also seen that the "rewarding" was near as well. Is this "rewarding" different from the "rewarding" and "coming" in 11:18, which is connected to the destruction of Jerusalem? Both David Chilton and Jay E. Adams see Revelation 11 as fulfilled. Chilton, before he

---

[150] I should note that Mathison also claims Revelation 11 speaks of the final judgment (1995, 131). However, to say his comments are self contradictory is a major understatement. He claims on the one hand that the kingdoms of the world became the kingdoms of the Lord in AD 70, but, the judgment of the living and the dead of the text is still future. He thus inserts a gap into the text where none is suggested or justified. This is the power of presuppositional theology. Indisputably, the time of the kingdoms becoming the kingdoms of the Lord and the time of the judgment are synchronous.

became a preterist, tried to dodge this by dividing this "judgment/rewarding/ resurrection" from the "final judgement at the Last Day" of the whole world! Thank God, before he passed away, he saw that such a division is a desperate attempt to separate what cannot be separated.

The basic reason why I call myself a "consistent" preterist is because I don't divide and piecemeal the Bible together to make it fit with the erroneous historical creeds on this point. I am not obligated to the creeds, but to Scripture. Creeds are fine, and they are logically necessary, but they "may err" as the Westminster Confession of Faith states (33:3). Some, however, have settled for man's word over God's, and it is this that I contend for.

It is obvious that the "time for judging the dead" is the same episode seen in Revelation 20:11-15. It is the same subject involved in I Corinthians 15. There, Paul wrote, "for the trumpet shall sound and the dead will be raised imperishable" (15:52). Also, he calls this the "last trumpet" (15:52). In John's vision, the trumpet is the seventh and last trumpet. One does not need to be a theologian and rocket scientist to see that they are talking about the exact same thing, about the exact same anticipated judgment to come upon Jerusalem "in this generation." The harmony is too simple to be missed.

But what happens after the "city" (Jerusalem) is destroyed in that chapter? John tells us: "The seventh angel sounded his trumpet" (11:15). What would happen after the trumpet is sounded? John tells us that heaven resounded in praise at the result of the destruction of the city (Jerusalem) and said, "We give thanks to you, Lord God Almighty, who is and who was, because you have taken your great power and have begun to reign" (11:17). Note that "is to come" is left off of the common tripartite formula ("who was, is, and is to come'), because this is the "coming" of the Lord! There is no "coming" after this!"[151]

In my estimation, this is an outstanding bit of exegesis, and cannot be overthrown or refuted.[152] And it proves beyond doubt that the judgment of the "living and the dead"-- the consummate judgment, *not a typological one*– occurred at the end of the Old Covenant world in AD 70.

---

[151] Sam Frost article:
(http://www.restorationgj.com/id45.htm)

[152] I could say a great deal about Frost's theology since abandoning Covenant Eschatology but will refrain. I will simply say I have seen nothing from his pen since his departure that has demonstrated any fallacy with his quote given here. As I write this, February, 2013, Frost and I are scheduled to have a formal pubic debate in January of 2014.

Revelation 11:15f posits the resurrection and the judgment of the living and the dead at the fall of Jerusalem in AD 70.

**Most of the leading Dominionists of the day agree!**

This puts them at odds with history and the creeds.

Most importantly, it refutes their idea that AD 70 was a type or shadow of the "real" judgment of the living and the dead. The judgment of the living and the dead of Revelation 11- as Frost irrefutably demonstrated– is the same judgment as Revelation 20.

**Thus, if Revelation 11 was fulfilled in AD 70 then Revelation 20 was fulfilled in AD 70.**

---

**Reason #14 -**
    **The End of the Millennium Arrived in AD 70**

---

Clearly, an in-depth study of the millennium is beyond the scope of this work. However, I want to make a few points that will, hopefully, demonstrate the problem with the traditional paradigms and establish the first century context of the millennium.[153]

Let me say this succinctly: martyr vindication is the key to a proper understanding of the millennium and when it was to end.

This is all but universally admitted by scholarship and established indisputably by the text of Revelation 20.

Gentry, commenting on Revelation 20, says, "The martyrs' deaths, (of Revelation 20, DKP) not only demand vindication, but explain and justify the judgments to follow."[154]

Dispensationalist Craig Blaising commenting on Revelation 20 as well says, "Revelation chapter 6 introduced the expectation that some justice would be executed by God on their behalf and they wait for

---

[153] For an excellent over-all study of the millennium see Joseph Vincent's *The Millennium: Past, Present or Future?* (Ardmore, Ok. JaDon Management Inc. 2012). Available from our websites, Amazon, Kindle, and other retailers.

[154] Kenneth Gentry, *Three Views of The Millennium and Beyond*, Stanley Gundry, Ed., (Grand Rapids, Zondervan, 1999)251.

that justice even as they are joined in waiting by subsequent martyrs. What John sees in Revelation 20 is the just vindication of believers slain for their faith, the fulfillment of them, or of the promises made by Christ himself."[155]

Aune, like many others, says Revelation 6 and Revelation 20 are parallel in their discussion of the martyrs.[156]

I could hardly agree more with these men– and many more could be cited, see Beale for instance.[157] However, I suggest it is fatal to any futurist view of Revelation 20 and the millennium to agree that vindication of the martyrs is the *crux interpretum* of the text.

It needs to be noted that Daniel 7 serves as the source of Revelation 20 and the promise of the vindication of the martyrs. Note this critical fact: no matter what else we might think of Revelation 20, since it is the fulfillment of Daniel 7, (with its promise of the coming of the Ancient of Days, the judgment, the vindication of the martyrs, etc.,) then the fulfillment of Revelation 20 cannot extend beyond the days of Rome.

Daniel 7 is clear that four kingdoms, with Rome being the final, are the temporal extent of the prophetic vista. Even the "little horn" comes up through and in the days of the last of the four kingdoms. There is simply no textual justification for extending the fulfillment of Daniel

---

[155] Craig Blaising in *Three Views of The Millennium and Beyond*, Stanley Gundry, series editor Darrel Bock general editor (Grand Rapids, Zondervan, 1999)222.

[156] David Aune, *Word Biblical Commentary, Revelation, Vol. 52c*, (Nashville, Nelson, 1998)1087+.

[157] Greg Beale, *New International Greek Testament Commentary, Revelation*, (Carlisle, PA., Paternoster, 1999, 1032f). This is really quite fatal to his paradigm.

beyond the days of Rome.

If this is true, and if the New Creation of Revelation 21f is the everlasting kingdom given to the saints at the time of judgment (Revelation 11:15f; Revelation 20:10f), then of logical necessity, the millennium simply cannot extend beyond the time of Rome. This, in a nutshell, negates all futurist views of eschatology.

> If Revelation 20:10f– the final vindication of all the martyrs– anticipated the fulfillment of Daniel 7, as most scholars believe, then one thing is inescapably true: Revelation 20 and the end of the millennium occurred in the days of the Roman Empire.
> **You cannot extend Daniel 7 – thus, Revelation 20 - beyond that time, without doing violence to the text.**

A second point to ponder is that Revelation 20 cannot be divorced from the earlier theme of the vindication of the martyrs. The vindication of the martyrs is one of, if not *the* most pervasive and dominant motifs in the entirety of Revelation and the totality of scripture. Note the following from Revelation.

Revelation 1 – "Behold he comes with the clouds, every eye shall see him and they shall look upon him whom they have pierced, even those who pierced him."

Revelation 6 – The souls of those under the altar crying out for vindication, "How long, O Lord?"

Revelation 7 – Tells us of the 144,000 who come out of the Great Tribulation. They are martyrs.

Revelation 12 -- The persecution of the seed of the man child and the destruction of Satan coming in just a little while.

Revelation 14 – Combines references to the martyrs, Babylon and the fulness of God's wrath, all elements linked with martyr vindication.

Revelation 16-19 -- The destruction of Babylon, the persecuting power, guilty of shedding all the blood of all the righteous shed on the earth, including that of the prophets.

Revelation 20 is clearly a recapitulation. It is a reiteration of the martyr theme of all of these chapters. Revelation 20, does not contain a separate promise of another vindication, of another body of martyrs different from that promised earlier in the apocalypse. I might add this is a major motif throughout the entire corpus of scripture.

What is more than evident in Revelation 20 – this is very critical – is that this motif is inextricably tied to the end of the millennium resurrection. It is likewise tied to the judgment. What is overlooked or ignored by the vast majority of commentators is *the motif of martyr vindication is inextricably tied to the judgment of Old Covenant Israel.*[158]
I suggest that we have from Jesus himself the definitive, final word on the time of the end of the millennium, i.e. when all the blood of all the martyrs would be vindicated.

"Woe to you, scribes and Pharisees, hypocrites! Because you build the tombs of the prophets and adorn the monuments of the righteous, 30 and say, 'If we had lived in the days of our fathers, we would not have been partakers with them in the blood of the prophets.' 31 "Therefore you are witnesses against yourselves that you are sons of those who

---

[158] As noted above, I presented a paper at Criswell College in Dallas, Tx., in October of 2012, on the "Preterist Perspective of the Millennium." That paper developed the unified doctrine of martyr vindication from the OT through Revelation 20, demonstrating the first century fulfillment– at the end of the millennium. For a free CD of that presentation, just pay postage. Contact me for a copy.

murdered the prophets. Fill up, then, the measure of your fathers' guilt. Serpents, brood of vipers! How can you escape the condemnation of hell? Therefore, indeed, I send you prophets, wise men, and scribes: some of them you will kill and crucify, and some of them you will scourge in your synagogues and persecute from city to city, that on you may come all the righteous blood shed on the earth, from the blood of righteous Abel to the blood of Zechariah, son of Berechiah, whom you murdered between the temple and the altar. Assuredly, I say to you, all these things will come upon this generation." (Matthew 23:29-37).

Jesus' words are clear, emphatic and undeniable: "all of the blood of all the righteous," all the way back to creation,[159] would be vindicated in the judgment of Old Covenant Jerusalem, in the first century.[160]

Consider this: Revelation 6 portrays the martyrs under the altar. Their prayer for vindication is the prayer of the martyrs in Luke 18, who cried out for vindication (Luke 18:1-8), and they were promised, "He shall avenge them speedily" (*en tachei*).[161] Their vindication would

---

[159] Matthew 23 effectively nullifies the argument that AD 70 was a "local judgment" of virtually no spiritual or universal significance. That judgment spanned the martyrs of the ages. Furthermore, Jesus's description of his parousia, and the world wide implications of it, are spelled out in Luke 21:25f.

[160] See my *Who Is This Babylon*, as well as *The Avenging of the Blood of the Apostles and Prophets* by Arthur Ogden for a full discussion of Jesus' words and their application to the entire subject of martyr vindication. Both books are available from my websites.

[161] Many commentators claim *en tachei* means "rapidity of action" as opposed to when the action would take place. Gentry effectively negates these claims in his *Before Jerusalem Fell*, 201,137f). Also, see my study of en tachei in

take place at the Great Day of the Lord (Revelation 6:12f).

The promise of imminent vindication in Revelation 6 is the promise of Matthew 23 and Luke 18. Thus, the vindication of the martyrs in Revelation 6 would take place at the judgment of Jerusalem in AD 70.

So, Revelation 6 and Revelation 20 are parallel, as the commentators agree. The martyrs of Revelation 6 would be avenged "in a little while" and this little while is delimited by "this generation" in Matthew 23. This effectively proves that the end of the millennium was in AD 70. That is, unless one can divorce Matthew 23 from Revelation. But this is simply untenable. Five quick facts establish this.

**First**, as just noted, the "little while" promise of vindication agrees with Jesus' promise of imminent vindication at the fall of Jerusalem.

**Second**, Revelation 6:12f, describes the Day of the Lord, the day of vindication, as the fulfillment of Isaiah 2:10f; 19f– the Day of the Lord when men would run to the hills from the Presence of the Lord. This could hardly describe an "end of time" event! Furthermore, Isaiah 4:4 describes this Day of the Lord as the time when the Lord would avenge the blood guilt of Jerusalem "by the spirit of fire and the spirit of judgment."[162]

---

my *Who Is This Babylon?* I examine every occurrence of the term in the NT and demonstrate that it clearly does not emphasize rapidity of action as opposed to imminence.

[162] Isaiah's prophecy is an extension of Deuteronomy 32. Moses foretold Israel's last days and said the blood of the martyrs would be avenged at that time (32:43). Significantly, in the fall of "Babylon" John directly echoes Deuteronomy 32:43. This has tremendous implications for the interpretation and dating of Revelation. See my *Who Is This Babylon?* for a detailed discussion.

So, Isaiah 2-4 predicted the "last days" Day of the Lord, a time when men could flee to the mountains. It would be a time of judgment on Israel (cf. Isaiah 3:13-24). It would be when the Lord avenged the blood of the martyrs (4:4).

What is so significant is that as Jesus was being led to his crucifixion, the women of Jerusalem were weeping for him. He said: "Daughters of Jerusalem, do not weep for Me, but weep for yourselves and for your children. For indeed the days are coming in which they will say, 'Blessed are the barren, wombs that never bore, and breasts which never nursed!' Then they will begin 'to say to the mountains, "Fall on us!" and to the hills, "Cover us!"' It is widely agreed that Jesus was citing Isaiah 2:19f (and par. Hosea 10:8). (Luke 23:28-30).

So, Jesus cited and applied Isaiah 2 to predict the judgment of Jerusalem for killing him, i.e. martyr vindication. Undeniably, Luke 23 is the same promise as in Matthew 23. John likewise cited the identical verses from Isaiah that Jesus applied to AD 70 (Revelation 6). What is the hermeneutical justification for claiming John had another set of martyrs, another Day of the Lord, another "last days," another vindication in mind?[163]

Simply stated, here is the argument:

Jesus applied the prophecy of Isaiah 2-4 and th prediction of the last days vindication of the martyrs at the Day of the Lord, to the AD 70 judgment of Jerusalem.

Revelation 6 cites the identical verses from Isaiah that Jesus applied to the impending judgment of Jerusalem– in John's promise of the imminent vindication of the martyrs at the Day of the Lord.

---

[163] See my full development of how Isaiah's prophecy is utilized in the NT in my *Who Is This Babylon?* There is a consistent application of Isaiah by Jesus, Paul and John.

Therefore, the vindication of the martyrs at the Day of the Lord in Revelation was to take place in the AD 70 judgment of Jerusalem.

**Third**, the Great Day of the Lord of Revelation 6:12f is the fulfillment of the mission and message of John, as Elijah. Remember, John was the fulfillment of Malachi 4:5-6, the prediction of the coming of Elijah before the Great and Terrible Day of the Lord. That Day would be when the Lord would come in judgment of Israel for violation of Torah (Malachi 3:5f) when no (evil) man could stand before Him at His presence (3:1-2). This would likewise be when the Lord opened His book of Remembrance, to make up the jewels of His crown. This is nothing less than the Great White Throne judgment when the "books were opened" (Revelation 20:10f).

So...
The Great Day of the Lord of Revelation 6– being the time of the vindication of the martyrs– is the time of Revelation 20.

The Great Day of the Lord of Revelation 6 is the Great Day of the Lord anticipated by John, as Elijah (Malachi 3-4).

John, as Elijah, said the Day of Judgment was near (Matthew 3:7-12).

Therefore, the Great Day of the Lord of Revelation 6– being the time of Revelation 20 and the end of the millennium– was near in the ministry of John.

**Fourth**, the Great White Throne judgment at the end of the millennium takes place when the full measure of martyrs was filled up. i.e. "the rest of the dead" corresponds perfectly with Revelation 6:10-11).[164]

---

[164] There are those who say the millennium began in AD 70 with the vindication of the martyrs E.g. James Jordan argued this in our public debate. DVDs are available from me. This is untenable. In Revelation 6 the martyrs were given

148

Notice that Jesus said the filling up of the measure of sin and suffering of the martyrs would be accomplished in his generation. See also Paul's discussion in which he all but quotes Jesus, in 1 Thessalonians 2:14-16. Babylon's cup of sin was now full when John wrote the Apocalypse. That cup contained the blood of the apostles and prophets, including the apostles of Jesus (Revelation 17:6; 18:20-24). Indeed, in her was found all of the blood shed on the earth– a direct echo of Matthew 23!

**Fifth**, the invariable testimony of the NT is that the vindication of the martyrs was imminent in the first century. Notice some of that testimony:

**Romans 8** - Sufferings of *the now present time* and the promise of the glory about to be revealed." Remember, DeMar and McDurmon[165] have shown the imminence of the text. Thus, the vindication of their martyrdom was near at the "glory about to be revealed."

**2 Corinthians 4:16f** - "Our light affliction which is but for a moment." The word rendered "affliction" is *thlipsis*, which seldom refers to the normal human experience. In the preponderant number of occurrences, it refers to persecution for the name of Christ.

**2 Thessalonians 1:7f** - "To you who are troubled, rest (relief, from

---

(royal) robes, which are equal to the thrones of chapter 20 *given at the initiation of the millennium.* After receiving the robes / thrones they had to wait a little while *for the Day of the Lord*, the time of their vindication. Very clearly, the Day of the Lord is the time of vindication, not the receiving of the robes / thrones which *initiated* the millennium. See Vincent's book on the Millennium, mentioned above for more on this critical aspect.

[165] McDurmon did not specifically posit an imminent fulfillment of Romans 8. However, his emphasis on the "now time" in Luke leads logically to the conclusion that Paul's "the now time" must likewise demand a first century fulfillment.

*anesis*) when the Lord Jesus is revealed from heaven."[166] Notice the perfect correspondence with Revelation 6– vindication at the Day of the Lord that was coming "in a little while."[167]

**Hebrews 10.34f** - "You took joyfully the spoiling of your goods... And now, in a very, very little while, the one who is coming will come, and will not delay" (v. 32-37).

DeMar says the time indicators surrounding the predictions of Jesus' coming "leave no room in this passage (2 Thessalonians 2:1) for a coming in the distant future" (1994, 318). In addition to 2 Thessalonians 2, DeMar lists the following texts which preclude a futurist application, due to the imminence found in them: Matthew 16:27-28 (set in a context of martyr vindication, DKP); Matthew 24:29f (also martyr vindication); 26:64 (clearly a text promising the vindication of Jesus' suffering); Hebrews 10:37; James 5:7-8; Revelation 2:5, 16; 3:11).

Of course, we have a right to ask how DeMar excludes Revelation 20 from that list, since it, like the others, is about the vindication of the martyrs, when the full number would be reached.

**James 5.6f** - Suffering of the saints is the context, and they were told "Be patient therefore, brethren, until the parousia" "The parousia has drawn nigh." "The judge is right at the Door." They were exhorted to look to the prophets who had suffered for examples of patience under

---

[166] See my *In Flaming Fire* book for an in-depth analysis of 2 Thessalonians 1. There could hardly be a more definitive, clear cut prediction of the first century parousia, in vindication of the martyrs.

[167] Beale gives a procrustean attempt (1999, 1018ff) to explain the "little while" of Revelation as in reality a long time. He says the "little while" must be viewed from God's perspective which of course says that although God was communicating to men, about events to take place on earth, He was being less than candid or forthright with the martyrs! Beale's explanation is just another example of the specious and desperate attempts by commentators to escape the clear cut language of scripture.

martyrdom.

**I Peter 1:5f; 4:1-17** - Suffering, martyrdom and imminent vindication permeates 1 Peter, as virtually all commentators agree. The parallels between 1 Peter and Revelation 6 are powerful and undeniable.

There is no question that martyrdom and the promise of imminent vindication permeates the Old Testament and New. We thus have the united testimony of Moses, Isaiah, Jesus, Paul, James and Peter all affirming martyr vindication would take place in Israel's last days in the judgment of Old Covenant Israel.

Revelation is saturated with this motif and there is no "near vindication" versus a "far vindication" with the exception of the giving of the robes / thrones, as they are then given the promise of imminent vindication. *There is no vindication of the martyrs isolated or divorced from Moses, Isaiah, Paul, James or Peter.*

So, the end of the millennium, Day of the Lord, Great White Throne Judgment, was near. This means of course, that AD 70 was not typological, or a foreshadowing of some greater, better, eschatological vindication.

To counter this, one would have to prove a number of things:
As we have suggested, it would have to be proven that the martyr vindication of Revelation 20 is to be divorced from the OT promises, from Jesus' promises in Matthew 23, Luke 18, etc., from Paul's discussion of imminent martyr vindication, from James and from Peter. Where is the textual, contextual justification for this claim? It simply does not exist.

So, the theme of martyr vindication in Revelation, in the OT and the rest of the New, is powerful and definitive. The full measure of the martyrs would be vindicated *at the end of the millennium*. And Jesus said all the blood, of all the righteous, of all the blood shed on the earth, would be avenged in the AD 70 judgment of Jerusalem. This demands that the end of the millennium judgment– the vindication of

151

the martyrs, was in AD 70. Thus, the Amillennial and Postmillennial claim that AD 70 was typological of the "real" end is false.

Unless it can be proven (*definitively*) that John's vision of the final vindication of the martyrs *at the end of the millennium* is to be divorced from the OT prophecies, from Jesus' teaching, from Paul, from Peter and from James– all who posited martyr vindication at AD 70- *then the end of the millennium arrived in AD 70.*

There is not a shred of evidence to suggest John wrote in total isolation from the rest of the Biblical testimony.

Thus, the end of the millennium was in AD 70.

---

**Reason #15 - If the Events of AD 70 Were Typological of a Future End of the Age, Then Christ Will Divorce and Destroy the Church, as an Unfaithful Bride That Has Become a Harlot and Will Marry Another Bride– Under (Another) New Covenant.**

---

We have exegetically demonstrated that it is untenable to say AD 70 was a foreshadowing of another end of the age. What we want to do now is to examine the logical implications of saying it was a foreshadowing of yet future events.

It is one thing to *claim* the end of the age events of the first century were typological of yet future events. It is another to actually examine what that means– and to prove the claim to be true. And the implications of such a doctrine are stunningly bad.

It is important here to understand what truly happened in the first century, in regards to the end of the age, by the admission of virtually all of those who say those events were typological. When we understand what took place and then examine the claim that AD 70 foreshadowed the ultimate fulfillment of those events, it will be quickly seen it is specious at best to say AD 70 was typological. In fact, to say AD 70 was typological is to suggest some things that are quite spurious, unscriptural and simply wrong.

To set the stage for understanding this, it needs to be understood *the Dominionists generally agree* that each of the (eschatological) elements listed below were fulfilled in AD 70.[168] Here is a short list of the eschatological tenets foretold by the OT:

√ The appearance of "Elijah" before the Great and Terrible Day of the Lord (Malachi 4:5-6).[169]

Mathison says Elijah was to come before "the end." Note his comments and how he (inadvertently I am sure) links the appearance of Elijah with the resurrection from the dead: "The promise of the coming of 'Elijah' ensure one more prophetic voice before the end came. (citing Baldwin). Before the coming of the great day of the Lord, God will send Elijah. Does this mean that God will send a reincarnation of the prophet Elijah or an Elijah-type prophet? The New Testament provides the answer by identifying John the Baptist as the one who fulfilled the prophecy (Matthew 11:13-14; 17:10-13). He is the one who prepared for the coming of Jesus the Messiah." (2009, 312)

Gentry likewise says John was the predicted Elijah: "Christ teaches his disciples that John the Baptist fulfills the Malachi prophecy covenantally, even though the Jews do not understand it. John introduces the restoration of all things, I. e. redemptive history's final phase in Christ's kingdom." (2009, 372).

---

[168] The list given here is taken from my *Like Father, Like Son* book, page 306. I have added additional points and bibliographic references.

[169] I am currently working on a book on the eschatological significance of John the Baptizer, as Elijah. In both Jewish expectation (as suggested by Mathison) and scripture, Elijah is clearly linked directly to the resurrection at the arrival of the kingdom. Jesus' undeniable identification of John as Elijah and John's pronouncement of the nearness of the kingdom serves as *prima facie* demonstration that the time of the resurrection was near in the first century. Needless to say, the implications of this are incredible.

√ Abomination of Desolation. (Gentry, 2009, 351+) says the prediction of the Abomination was fulfilled in the Jewish War of 66-70 AD. DeMar and Mathison (*Age*, 2009, 375) agree. McDurmon says Jesus' prediction of the Abomination, along with the separation of the wheat and tares (Matthew 13): "describes the then soon coming end of that old age and the destruction of its children, and the beginning of the gathering in of the true children of God's kingdom. It should not be understood as teaching anything beyond this."[170]

Note how McDurmon says it is inappropriate to apply those elements to any time or events beyond AD 70. Yet, in our public debate in July, 2012, McDurmon claimed the proper hermeneutic– *and it is essential for his eschatology*-- is to understand that prophecy is fulfilled over and over, again and again!

Note McDurmon's problem here:
The end of the old age and destruction of its children— the gathering of the true children of God into His kingdom - i.e. resurrection, DKP —occurred in AD 70 and "should not be understood as teaching anything beyond this"—McDurmon.

But, McDurmon says AD 70 was typological of another, yet future, end of the age and gathering of the true children of God into His kingdom, i.e. the "real" resurrection.

Therefore, McDurmon contradicts his own hermeneutic and creates an unknown, un-Biblical eschatology.

This is clearly problematic for McDurmon and other postmillennialists. How can you affirm repeatedly that the end of the age events of AD 66-70 were typological of the coming end of the age

---

[170] Joel McDurmon, *Jesus V Jerusalem: A Commentary on Luke 9:51- 20:26, Jesus Lawsuit Against Jerusalem,* (Atlanta, Ga., American Vision, 2011)49.

and harvest, but then turn around and say the end of the age events Jesus foretold, "should not be understood as teaching anything beyond this"?

√ The Great Tribulation. Gentry says "Copious, clear and compelling evidence demonstrates that the great tribulation occurs in the first century" (2009, 356). Mathison likewise says: "There is no end time tribulation. Jesus' prophecy about tribulation in Matthew 24 was fulfilled between AD 30 and AD 70. That fulfillment should give us confidence that His promise to return again is true" (1995,144). In stark contrast, Gary North says that at the end of the millennium, "The devil will be loosed for a little season at the end of time, meaning his power over the nations returns to him in full strength (Rev. 20:3)."[171]

√ The Man of Sin, i.e. the Beast of Revelation. DeMar says Nero was the beast of Revelation, the Man of Sin of 2 Thessalonians.[172] Gentry concurs.[173] In fact, most Dominionists agree.

√ The resurrection of the dead (Isaiah 25:6-8;[174] Daniel 12:2[175]). As

---

[171] Gary North, *Dominion and Common Grace*, (Tyler, Tx. Institute for Christian Economics, 1987)170.

[172] Gary DeMar, *Last Days Madness, Obsession of the Modern Church*, (Atlanta, GA., American Vision, 1994)205+.

[173] Kenneth Gentry, *The Beast of Revelation*, (Tyler, Tx., Institute for Christian Economics, 1989).

[174] It is interesting to say the least Gentry does not even list Isaiah 25-27 in *Dominion*. One can but wonder why.

[175] Gentry, *(Dominion*, 2009, 538): "Daniel appears to be presenting Israel as a grave site under God's curse; Israel as a corporate body is in the dust (Daniel 12:2; cp. Ge. 3:14,

noted, in our formal debate, McDurmon stated repeatedly that even the resurrection of 1 Corinthians 15 and Revelation 20 had "a fulfillment" in AD 70.

✔ The passing of "heaven and earth" (Isaiah 51; 65; 66).[176]

✔ The arrival of the New Creation (Isaiah 65-66; Revelation 21-22).[177]

✔ The arrival of the New Jerusalem (Isaiah 52; 65:13f).

✔ The Messianic Marriage (Hosea; Isaiah 62) at the coming of the Bridegroom.

---

19). In this he follows Ezekiel's pattern in his vision of the dry bones, which represents Israel's 'death' in the Babylonian dispersion (Ezekiel 37). In Daniel's prophecy many will awaken, as it were, during the great tribulation to suffer the full fury of divine wrath, while others will enjoy God's grace in receiving everlasting life"

[176] Jonathin Seriah, says, "The 'heaven and earth' of Judaism that passed away in the first century (2 Peter 3:10; Revelation 21:1) were 'obsolete and growing old' (Hebrews 8:13)" (*The End of All Things*, (Moscow, Idaho, Canon Press, 1999)54).

[177] Gentry, *Dominion*, (2009, 367): "John sees the New Jerusalem coming down out of heaven to earth in the establishment of Christianity (Revelation 21:1-2). This was the heavenly city that Abraham ultimately sought beyond the temporal (and typical) Promised land (Hebrews 11:10, 16). (2009, 147). He adds: "The Heavenly Jerusalem is the bride of Christ that comes down from God to replace the earthly Jerusalem (Rev 21:2-5) in the first century (Rev 1:1, 3; 22:6, 10). With the shaking and destruction of the old Jerusalem in AD 70, the heavenly (recreated) Jerusalem replaces her"

✔ The Messianic Temple (Isaiah 4; Ezekiel 37; Zechariah 6:13).[178]

✔ The Messianic Banquet (at the time of the resurrection- Isaiah 25; 65). McDurmon is adamant, in his writings, that Abraham, Isaac and Jacob sat down at the Banquet in AD 70 when the Old Covenant "sons of the kingdom" were cast out (2011, 64).[179]

✔ The judgment coming of the Lord (Isaiah 40:10f; 62:10f ☛ Matthew 16:27-28). (Gentry, 2009, 342).

---

[178] *Gentry, (Dominion*, 2009 342) says of Matthew 8:11– "In fact, the dark clouds of the 'day of the Lord' in AD 70 hang over much of the New Testament. God is preparing to punish His people Israel, remove the temple system, and re-orient redemptive history from one people and land to all peoples through the earth (Matthew 8:10-11– 21:43)."

[179] In our debate, I continually pressed McDurmon that his affirmation Abraham had sat down at the Messianic Banquet foretold by Isaiah 25 is nothing less than admission that the end of the millennium resurrection has been fulfilled. In Isaiah, the Banquet and the resurrection are inextricably tied to each other. In Paul, the resurrection of Isaiah 25 was his resurrection hope (1 Corinthians 15:54-56). McDurmon's only attempt at a response was to claim there is no proof Isaiah foretold the end of the millennium resurrection because the word "final" is not present! This is patently nothing but desperation.

✔ The End of the Age.[180] DeMar agrees with Gentry,[181] as does McDurmon.[182] The end of the age arrived in AD 70.

---

[180] "The change of the age is finalized and sealed at the destruction of Jerusalem; allusions to the A.D. 70 transition abound: 'Assuredly, I say to you that there are some standing here who will not taste of death till they see the kingdom of God present with power '(Mark 9:1) (Kenneth L. Gentry and Thomas Ice, *The Great Tribulation Past Or Future?*, (Grand Rapids, MI: Kregel Publications, 1999)63.

[181] "Jesus' coming to destroy Jerusalem represented the passing of the Old Covenant." Gary DeMar, *Last Days Madness* (Revised) (Atlanta, GA., American Vision, 1994)157; "The Old Covenant came to an end with the destruction of the temple in AD 70" ( 1994, 56).

[182] Commenting on Hebrews 8:13, McDurmon says, "As he wrote, in his time, the Old was becoming obsolete and was ready to vanish away. It has not yet been completely wiped out, but was certainly in its dying moments. It died in AD 70, when the symbol and ceremonies of that Old System– the Temple and the sacrifices– were completely destroyed by the Roman armies. This was the definitive moment when 'this age' of Jesus and Paul ended and completely gave way to their 'age to come.' This, of course, is exactly why Jesus tied 'the end of the age' to His prophecy of the destruction of the Temple." (2011, 47).

✔ The "Great Commission"[183] (Isaiah 11; 65).[184]

The Postmillennial world is "bi-polar" when it comes to the Great Commission. For instance, Mathison says on the one hand, "the end does not come until the missionary task is completed. Since the missionary task has not yet been completed, even in our day, the implication would seem to be that the end in view here is the end of redemptive history" (2009, 373). However, in another place he says, "Jesus said the Gospel will be preached in all the whole world. Was that fulfilled before AD 70? Scripture says yes."[185]

---

[183] See my *We Shall Meet Him In The Air, The Wedding of the King of kings*, where I document from the early church fathers that they believed virtually everyone of the tenets listed here were indeed fulfilled in the first century. It is undeniable that the majority of the early fathers believed the World Mission had been fulfilled.

[184] As suggested, there is tremendous ambivalence in the Postmillennial world about the Great Commission. When debating the dispensationalists, they affirm the first century fulfillment of the Mission. McDurmon says, "Saul is converted, and that of course means that the gospel will reach the entire inhabited world in the lifetimes of those very disciples." *Jesus V Jerusalem*, (Powder Springs, GA, American Vision, 2011)31. However, when developing their Postmillennial world view, they insist that Matthew 28:18-20 has not yet been fulfilled. See Gentry: http://againstdispensationalism.com/2011/12/the-great-tribulation-in-progressive-dispensationalism-by-ken-gentry. In effect they create two World Missions, one fulfilled, the other unfulfilled. See my *Into All the World, Then Comes The End*, for a refutation of the idea of two World Missions.

[185] Keith Mathison, *Dispensationalism, Rightly Dividing the People of God?*, (Phillipsburg, NJ, P&R Publishing, 1995)141.

Gentry is just as "double minded" when it comes to the World Mission. In his debate with Thomas Ice, Gentry appealed to Romans 1:8, 10:18, Colossians 1:6 and 1:23 to affirm the first century fulfillment of Matthew 24:14 (1999, 43-45). However, when positing the Postmillennial view, he says the World Mission remains *unfulfilled*.[186] Gentry and other postmillennialists thus create a doctrine of two Great Commissions. In fact, the creation of two World Mission mandates is absolutely *critical* to the Dominionist paradigm. But this is entirely unscriptural.[187]

As one looks at the list of these predicted events it is undeniably true they are all fundamentally *eschatological* in nature. Keep in mind that Gentry acknowledges the OT perspective was these things would "fully arrive" at the end of the Old Covenant age– not typologically. Gentry is correct. That is, the Old Covenant prophets, as noted above, never predicted two end times eras, two last days Days of the Lord, two kingdoms, two resurrections, etc. There was but one eschatological hope, to be fulfilled when Old Covenant Israel would be destroyed.

With these tenets before us, and with documentation that the Dominionists– at least many of them-- affirm the first century fulfillment of each of them, let's take a closer look at the implications of saying AD 70 was typological of a future eschaton.

Consider that with few exceptions (e.g. Gary North) there is consensus, at least among the men cited, that the Man of Sin, the Abomination of Desolation and the Great Tribulation all occurred in

---

186

http://againstdispensationalism.com/2011/12/the-great-tribulati on-in-progressive-dispensationalism-by-ken-gentry/

[187] See my *Into All The World, Then Comes the End*, for a complete refutation of the Two Commission view. Available from Amazon, my websites and other retailers.

the first century. But, with this in mind, let me give the list again, taking note of how the Dominionist "pick and choose" what is typological and what is not.

√ The appearance of "Elijah" before the Great and Terrible Day of the Lord (Malachi 4:5-6).
Typological? No. I have not found even one Dominionists who posits a yet future appearance of another Elijah, whether the "real" one, or another one ministering in the spirit and power of Elijah like John.

√ Abomination of Desolation.
Typological? No. I have not found any Dominionists who posits a yet future Abomination of Desolation. (Some amillennialists do however, e.g. Riddlebarger–2006, 70).

√ The Great Tribulation.
Typological? No, although as we have seen, Gary North does posit another future Great Tribulation prior to the end of the millennium. However, so far as I can determine, and as noted above, this is not the dominant view among postmillennialists.

√ The Man of Sin, i.e. the Beast of Revelation.
Typological? No.[188] Gentry, DeMar (1994, 195ff) and McDurmon reject the idea that the first century anti-christs were types of a final, yet future anti-christ.

✔ The resurrection of the dead (Isaiah 25:6-8;[189] Daniel 12:2).
Typological? Yes!

---

[188] Amillennialist Kim Riddlebarger does believe the first century anti-christs were typological of a coming Antichrist at the end of time. *(The Man of Sin*, Grand Rapids, Baker, 2006)69.

[189] It is interesting to say the least Gentry does not even list Isaiah 25-27 in *Dominion*. One can but wonder why.

As I have noted, in our formal debate, McDurmon stated repeatedly that even the resurrection of 1 Corinthians 15 and Revelation 20 had "a fulfillment" in AD 70.

✔ The passing of "heaven and earth" (Isaiah 51; 65; 66). Typological? Yes.[190]

✔ The arrival of the New Creation (Isaiah 65-66; Revelation 21-22). Typological? Yes.

✔ The arrival of the New Jerusalem (Isaiah 52; 65:13f). Typological? Yes.

✔ The Messianic Marriage (Hosea; Isaiah 62) at the coming of the Bridegroom.
Typological? Well, this is where it gets *really* sticky, as we shall see momentarily.

✔ The Messianic Temple (Isaiah 4; Ezekiel 37; Zechariah 6:13). Typological? There is a lot of silence about this issue.

---

[190] Once again we see the ambivalence in the Dominionist world. Some (e.g. Gentry) say 2 Peter 3 predicts the end of material creation. However, this is unsettling to those like McDurmon who believe the kingdom must be established on earth, in time, at the end of the current Christian age. Many Dominionists, even Gentry, see the passing of "heaven and earth" in Revelation 21 as the passing of a covenantal creation, i.e. Old Covenant Israel, not literal creation. It is not too much to say that the Dominionists are "all over the map" when it comes to the various prophecies of the passing of "heaven and earth." The brief statement is that they see the passing of the Old Covenant "heaven and earth" as a foreshadowing of the passing of the New Covenant creation. Oh, but, wait, they take contradictory views on whether the New Covenant will ever come to an end! Confusing? Yes.

✔ The Messianic Banquet (at the time of the resurrection- Isaiah 25; 65).

Typological? A mixed bag here since on the one hand, as we have seen, McDurmon as well as Gentry believe the sitting down at the Banquet occurred in AD 70. Well, per Isaiah 25, that Banquet would be at the resurrection– which is the resurrection of 1 Corinthians 15. And remember, that McDurmon posits "a fulfillment" of 1 Corinthians 15 in AD 70. So, consistency and logic would seem to demand that yes, they do see the Messianic Banquet as typological.

✔ The judgment coming of the Lord (Isaiah 40:10f; 62:10f ☛ Matthew 16:27-28).

Typological? Yes.

✔ The End of the Age.

Typological? Yes. Amillennialists clearly see the future end of the world, typified by the events of the first century.[191]

---

[191] Greg Beale, "If the OT usage of this kind of language (Joel 2- DKP) is determinative for Peter, then here also the wording connotes the end of one kingdom and the emergence of another. The kingdom ending is, of course, Israel, but this time it is her definitive end. Rome would destroy Jerusalem in AD 70. Joel's language of the earth's destruction in Acts 2 is also appropriate as a figurative portrayal of the temple's destruction, since, as we have seen so often earlier, the temple itself and its parts symbolized the cosmos. We observed that when the temple veil was torn, it was symbolic of the beginning destruction of the old creation." (Beale, *Temple*, 2005, 214). Also, "The events of AD 70 point typologically to the events at the very end of the world." (*Temple*, p. 213, n. 29). We have here the prediction– *logically–* of the destruction of the *church*. The end of the world / age in AD 70 was not the end of the material cosmos, but the end of a covenant world. *So, why does not the end of one covenant world not foreshadow the end of another covenant world, instead of typifying the end of time and*

164

✔ The "Great Commission" (Isaiah 11; 65).
Typological?[192] Yes.

It takes little to see how arbitrary and capricious the Dominionists are in their application of typology in regard to the first century end of the age events.

> The Dominionists are totally arbitrary and capricious in their application of "typology" to the end of the age events of the first century. They simply dismiss some events (i.e. John as Elijah, the antichrists, the Abomination) as foreshadowings, while insisting other elements (the World Mission, the judgment, resurrection and parousia) were in fact typological. What is their proof? They give none.

What I want to do now is demonstrate how the Dominionists' and amillennialists' view of those first century events as types and foreshadowings is untenable. I will focus primarily on the idea of the Wedding and the New Covenant themes, although much could be said of virtually *all* of the other tenets.

To appreciate the problem for the "AD 70 was a type" hermeneutic of the postmillennialists especially, one must understand their view of the Old Covenant and the Wedding of the Lord.

So, what happened in AD 70 per the Dominionist view of the marriage

---

*space?*

[192] Amillennialist Riddlebarger, (2006, 70) does not seem to see a first century typological fulfillment of the World Mission. Instead, he says in Matthew 24:4-13 Jesus discussed first century events but then in v. 14, "he immediately leaps ahead to the time of the end."

and Old Covenant?

Gentry, DeMar, McDurmon Jordan[193] and a host of other Dominionists believe the following:
God was married to Old Covenant Israel.
Torah, the Law of Moses, was the marriage covenant.
Just as the ten northern tribes committed spiritual adultery and God divorced her (Malachi 2), even so in the last days, Judah, who was still married to the Lord, would likewise be unfaithful.
The book of Revelation is the story of the unfaithful wife, (Gentry, 2009, 384)[194] and the divorce,[195] but, then, the full establishment of the New (Marriage) Covenant, when Christ married his New Bride, in AD 70.

Remember this quote from Gentry, cited earlier in this work:"John sees the New Jerusalem coming down out of heaven to earth in the establishment of Christianity (Revelation 21:1-2). This was the heavenly city Abraham ultimately sought beyond the temporal (and

---

[193] Remember that Jordan is not a Postmillennialist. He is a Reformed Amillennialist, yet, he espouses many of the Dominionist views.

[194] At the time of this writing, Gentry is working to finalize a tome on Revelation in which he will focus, per the reports, on the marriage, divorce and remarriage motif in the Apocalypse.

[195] Cf. McDurmon, (2011, 158) commenting on the Wedding parable of Matthew 22 and the destruction of the wicked guests: "out with the old whore Jerusalem, and in with the new saintly bride– arrayed in the fine linen of 'the righteousness of the saints' (Revelation 19:7-7; cf. who had righteousness in Romans 10:3-4).'"

typical) Promised land (Hebrews 11:10, 16). (2009, 147).[196]

He adds: "The Heavenly Jerusalem is the bride of Christ that comes down from God to replace the earthly Jerusalem (Rev 21:2-5) in the first century (Rev 1:1, 3; 22:6, 10). With the shaking and destruction of the old Jerusalem in AD 70, the heavenly (recreated) Jerusalem replaces her" (2009, 367).

Okay, a brief refresher. Most postmillennialists believe the following:
Old Covenant Israel foreshadowed New Covenant Israel.
Old Covenant Jerusalem foreshadowed the New Covenant Jerusalem.
The Old Covenant typified the New Covenant.
The Old Covenant Marriage foreshadowed the New Covenant Marriage.
And of course, as we have seen, the end of the Old Covenant age and attendant events of the first century foreshadowed the coming future consummation.

Well, then, if those Old Covenant realities point to the future, then we have every right to ask the following questions:

✤ Will the church- the Bride of Christ he married in AD 70- become an "old whore" to borrow McDurmon's words, an unfaithful wife—like the typological Old Covenant Israel / Judah did? If not, why not?

Needless to say, if the Dominionists say the apostasy of the first covenant bride is typological of the second, there is no logical reason

---

[196] In Hebrews 11, the heavenly city and the "better resurrection" are directly connected to the Abrahamic promises and hope. So, for Gentry to affirm the fulfillment of the Abrahamic promise of the New Jerusalem is nothing less than an admission the "better resurrection" took place in AD 70. And of course this raises the question, if the Abrahamic promise of the better resurrection was fulfilled, then what "better resurrection" still awaits fulfillment?

167

to suggest the bride that was married in AD 70 will not commit adultery just like the first wife. And, if this is true, the entire Dominionist paradigm that the world– and the church's righteous influence in the world– will continually get stronger and stronger is nullified.

---

If the Postmillennial claim that AD 70 was typological of another end of the age is true, **this totally falsifies Dominionism!**

The end of the age in AD 70 was the divorce of an unfaithful, harlot wife, the passing of that marriage covenant and the creation of a New Covenant with a New Bride.

If AD 70 was typological of our future therefore, the church will not get better and better, increasing her righteous influence in the world.

She will get worse and worse until her husband is forced to divorce her and then marries another Bride!

You cannot logically claim that the events of AD 70 were typological without demanding this very scenario!

---

❖ So, will the New Covenant Bride become unfaithful, becoming a harlot, just like the first wife, fulfilling the typological import of the first wife? If not, then the typology is broken.

❖ Will the Lord divorce the church at the end of the Christian age, as he (typologically) divorced Old Covenant Israel?

❖ Will the New (Marriage) Covenant be annulled and broken, as the first marriage covenant was?

❖ Will the Lord make another New (Marriage) Covenant, at the end of the current (covenant) age?

168

It is impossible to over-emphasize the centrality of covenant in regard to the end of the age events. Very clearly if the end of the Old Covenant was the focus of AD 70, as posited by Dominionists, and if AD 70 was typological of the real end, then of logical necessity AD 70 was typological of the end of Christ's unending, never to be shaken New Covenant.

You cannot logically say the end of the age in AD 70 was typological of the future end of the age, without at least considering the *reasons* for the end of that Old Covenant age. That Old Covenant age– as even Jordan noted– was supposed to end because of its sin, deficiency and failure. So, again, if AD 70 was in fact typological of the end of the current age, does this not suggest that the current age– the age of Christ's church– must be brought to an end for the same reasons? (Go back and read our comments on the unending New Covenant).

❖ Will the Lord marry another Bride, at the end of the current marriage covenant?

If as Gentry claims, the Bride of Christ fully supplanted Old Covenant Israel in AD 70,[197] and if the prophets foretold the *full arrival* of the Wedding at the end of the Old Covenant age, then *there is not another Wedding to be anticipated at the end of the Christian age.*

But, this is especially troublesome for Gentry, because he applies

---

[197] Consider: Gentry says the OT prophets foretold the full arrival of the New Creation at the end of the Old Covenant age. He says the New Covenant bride "fully supplanted" the Old in AD 70. This logically demands that we are not therefore, still waiting for the full arrival of the New Creation. See my *We Shall Meet Him In The Air, The Wedding of the King of kings*, for a full critique of Gentry's comments.

Matthew 25:1f to Christ's "end of human history" parousia.[198] Furthermore, Matthew 25 is critical to Gentry's futurism, for he uses the story of the Bridegroom to justify the 2000 year delay of the parousia.

Gentry says, "His return not been imminent since the ascension"; "The New Testament teaches, however, that the Lord's glorious, bodily return will be in the *distant* and *unknowable* future. It has not been *imminent* and will not be *datable*. Theologically 'distinctive to (Postmillennialism) is the *denial* of the imminent physical return' of Christ." – "Jesus clearly taught: 'While the bridegroom was delayed, they all slumbered and slept (Matthew 25:5). For the kingdom of heaven is like a man traveling to a far country, who called his own servants and delivered his goods to them... After a long time, the Lord of those servants came and settled accounts with them (Matthew 25:14, 19). There is no expectation here of an any-moment return– there is quite the opposite." *(*1992, 331).

So, Gentry appeals to Matthew 25 to justify the so far 2000 year "delay" in the coming of Christ[199] (and in the text it is clearly a "delay"). Yet, that parable is about Christ coming *to marry his bride*! So, this means Gentry has a Wedding of Christ in AD 70, when he divorced the Old Covenant, unfaithful, harlot wife, and, he has another

---

[198] There is growing division in the Postmillennial world in regard to the Olivet Discourse. Historically, leading postmillennialists have posited a divided discourse, claiming Jesus predicted both the AD 70 end of the age, but, at v. 36 (or thereabouts) he changed subjects and began discussing the end of time and the physical cosmos. Boettner, Gentry and others still hold to this. However, DeMar, McDurmon and others now say the entirety of the Olivet Discourse speaks of AD 70.

[199] Other Dominionists reject Gentry's appeal to Matthew 25 for a 2000 year delay in the parousia. As we have seen, McDurmon applies the Wedding parable to AD 70.

marriage at some point in the future, i.e. at the end of time.

McDurmon *seems* to imply this as well, although his words are a bit ambiguous: "They (the Jews, DKP) had missed their opportunity, not having their lamps lit. They lost all future inheritance, and were left no better than adulterers, as far as *that particular Bridegroom* was concerned." (Emphasis mine. What in the world does "that particular Bridegroom" mean?) To say this is troublesome is a huge understatement.

I want to further emphasize the problem Gentry's comments pose for the Dominionists who agree with him.

**Christ did not simply *betroth* the church in AD 70– he married her.**

**But, the marriage was to be at the Second Coming (Matthew 25:1f– which Gentry applies to "the end of human history").**

**Therefore, the Second Coming when Christ married (not a betrothal), was in AD 70– or else we must have two brides, and two weddings in view.**

Look what this means for the "AD 70 was a type of the real end" view.

**The events of AD 70 were a typological foreshadowing of the "real" end of the age.**

**Christ married his bride, consummating the betrothal, in AD 70.**

**Therefore, Christ will marry his bride– again- or will marry another bride, at the "real" end.**

Very clearly, *another bride / Wedding is demanded* in Gentry's construct. If Christ married the church in AD 70 *he did not merely betroth her*. Thus, since Gentry posits the marriage of Matthew 25 at

171

the end of the Christian age this logically demands another bride, another wedding.

In addition, it is important to emphasize again that Gentry not only posits the Wedding in AD 70, he believes this was the time when Christ *divorced Old Covenant Judah, the unfaithful harlot bride!* So, if AD 70 was typological of the real end, here is what we have:

**The events of AD 70 were typological of the real end of the age- the end of the Christian age.**

**In AD 70 Christ divorced an unfaithful, covenant bride who had become a harlot.**

**Therefore, at the "real end" i.e. the end of the Christian age, Christ divorces his current bride, i.e. the church, who has become an unfaithful harlot wife.**

Now, there is absolutely no scriptural evidence to support such a view. And, it is to be noted, this scenario totally falsifies the "optimistic" world view of the triumphant church that will ostensibly get better and better per the Dominionists.

I think the reader can see the Wedding motif is tremendously troublesome for the Dominionist view of AD 70 being typological of yet future events. And the problem is exacerbated by the fact the Wedding is no tangential, minor element of eschatological doctrine. It is *foundational.* Thus, it is clearly untenable to say the Wedding would not be part of the typological significance of AD 70.

We cited Gentry earlier how he rejects the Dispensational Double Fulfillment paradigm. We promised to return to his work, so, we give here Gentry's three reasons for rejecting the Double Fulfillment of the anti-christ, Abomination, Tribulation prophecies– all the while saying the events of AD 70 were, nonetheless, typological.

172

1.) "The beast prophecy is set in a very clear context calling for its *soon* fulfillment."

2.) "We really stretch credibility if we argue that all the many details of the beast (and why not of all of Revelation?) are to be fulfilled in incredible detail *again* later."

3.) "The beast belongs to the first century Roman era, irrespective of the many time qualifiers scattered throughout Revelation."[200]

I would suggest that Gentry's reasons for rejecting the Double Fulfillment hermeneutic provide *strong reasons* for why we should likewise reject the idea AD 70 was typological of a yet future end of the age. Consider the following:

1.) The end of the age, judgment and resurrection prophecies of the New Testament are "set in a very clear context calling for its *soon* fulfillment." This is undeniable.[201] The imminence of these events is set forth in a variety of ways, utilizing different words.[202] It is only

---

[200] Kenneth Gentry, *Perilous Times A Study in Eschatological Evil*, (Texarkana, Covenant Media Press, 1999)133f.

[201] See my *Who Is This Babylon* for a full discussion of the objective nature of the imminence of the end in the NT epistles.

[202] It is fascinating- not to mention troubling- to see some Postmillennialists now hedging on the Biblical statements of the imminence of the end. In our debate Joel McDurmon introduced some texts he claimed indicate a problem with the imminence factor. This in spite of the fact in his book *Jesus V Jerusalem*, he constantly emphasizes the imminence factor and audience relevance of those statements, claiming to ignore it is bad hermeneutic. We concur of course, but, increasingly, Dominionists, entrapped by their own past

173

because of preconceived ideas about the nature of the end that has caused Bible students to created "inventive" ways to escape the force of these multitudinous statements.

> Gentry rejects the Double Fulfillment of Elijah, the anti-christ, Abomination and Tribulation prophecies because of the language of imminence. Yet, he says the "end of the age," the judgment and resurrection- that were "at hand" and coming "quickly" in the NT- were typological of yet future events!
> If the presence of John as Elijah and the imminence of the anti-christ negates a double fulfillment, then surely, the nearness of the end of the age, the judgment and resurrection likewise falsify the idea of "multiple fulfillments" of the end of the age and resurrection! This means AD 70 was "the end of the age"; it was "the judgment"; it was "the resurrection."
> **Gentry's hermeneutic has falsified his futurism.**

2.) I would suggest, "We really stretch credibility if we argue that all the many details of the end of the age, the judgment and resurrection are to be fulfilled in incredible detail *again* later."

---

insistence that we honor the time statements now want to equivocate when debating or discussing preterism. For a good discussion of audience relevance see DeMar's article. After you read it, apply what he says to the eschatological texts of the NT and ask how DeMar, McDurmon, et. al, can argue so logically and convincingly on audience relevance and time statements in the Olivet Discourse and then turn around and totally ignore or distort audience relevance and temporal indicators in the other texts. DeMar's article can be found here:
https://americanvision.org/5672/timing-and-audience-relevance-and-interpreting-the-bible/

I am confident Gentry, DeMar, McDurmon, et. al. would insist "all the many details " of the end are not, in fact, "to be fulfilled in incredible detail *again* later." They would argue– precisely as do the Dispensationalists – only *some* of the end time events are to be fulfilled again.

The key question is, what is the hermeneutical principle whereby the Dominionist can justify saying. "Well, there will not be another future anti-christ, Abomination of Desolation, or Great Tribulation, but, there will be another parousia, judgment and resurrection at the end of the age"?

> The key question is, what is the hermeneutical principle whereby the Dominionist can justify saying. "Well, there will not be another future Elijah, another anti-christ, Abomination of Desolation or Great Tribulation, but, there will be another parousia, judgment and resurrection"? Do the Dominionists just get to say: "Because I say so"? Or do we not have the right to demand exegetical, logical *evidence*?

It should be noted here that in Jewish thought, and in scripture, there is one organic end times drama. The (implied) suggestion of the Dominionists that John as Elijah, the anti-christs, Abomination and Tribulation are somehow, someway, non-essential to the end time drama and therefore not typological-- is specious.

For instance, the tribulation and the resurrection are absolutely inextricably tied together in Isaiah 25-27 and Daniel 12.[203] So, if, as

---

[203] It is a strange thing to witness what is happening in the Postmillennial world in regard to Daniel 12.
Historically, there is no doubt the unquestioned view is that Daniel foretold the final, "end of human history" resurrection.
However, when true preterists began noting and emphasizing

does Gentry and McDurmon, you posit "a" resurrection in AD 70 but claim it is typological of the "real" resurrection, then logically, this would suggest the Tribulation, immediately preceding the resurrection in *Torah*, would likewise be a foreshadowing of the true Great Tribulation[204]– which of course would be prompted by the man of sin and the Abomination!

The point here cannot be over-emphasized. Since the end time events are all part of the *one organic story* in scripture, then to posit any part of that narrative as typological would seem to logically demand that all of the constituent elements of the drama were equally typological. The Dominionist rejection of this consistency is, to say the least, disingenuous.

Consider the New Heaven and Earth for instance. Many

---

that Daniel 12:7 undeniably posits resurrection at the end of Old Covenant Israel's age, we are seeing an amazing turn around! From Gentry, to Frost, to McDurmon, to Mathison, there has been what can only be described as a frantic, desperate attempt to find some explanation– any explanation– of Daniel 12 that will allow them to maintain their futurist eschatology. Amazingly, postmillennialists, who are mostly Reformed, and thus creedal, now feel no reservation in rejecting the historical, creedal view of Daniel 12, (all the while condemning true preterists for being non-creedal, of course). They now freely apply Daniel to AD 70. Yet, they totally ignore the fact that Daniel and Isaiah 25-27, which serves as one of the sources of Paul's resurrection doctrine, *are directly parallel*. So, if they "surrender" Daniel 12 to AD 70, then *analogia scriptura* would logically demand that they have surrendered Isaiah and thus 1 Corinthians 15, to AD 70.

[204] This is precisely what is seen in Revelation 20, is it not? Is not the Tribulation tied directly to the resurrection at the end of the millennium? How then can the Dominionists say the first century Tribulation did not foreshadow another one, but claim the first century resurrection did typify another one?

176

Postmillennialists say Isaiah 65 and the New Creation foretold there came in AD 70. This being true, note *what had to happen* in order to bring in that New Creation: A.) God destroyed a covenant people. B.) He created *another* covenant people. C) He gave that New People a New Name (v. 8-17).

So, if those end of the age events are *typological of the future*, then surely at the end of the current Christian age, *God will destroy the current covenant people and create a New People with a New Name.* If not, why not?

It simply will not do to talk generically of the finer details, or "all the many details" as if those details were not integral to the end time drama. In Isaiah– and throughout scripture– *the very reason* for the end of the Old Covenant age, and *the very reason* for the New was due to the apostasy of the Old Covenant people, the insufficiency of that Old Covenant and the bringing in of a better creation.

These are not tangential details. They are the core, foundational *critical* "details." Thus, if AD 70 was typological, this means the church will be destroyed, and a New People with a New Name and New Covenant– surpassing the Gospel of Christ– will be created. You cannot argue that AD 70 and attendant events were typological without logically demanding that what happened in AD 70 will be fulfilled in a greater manner at the end of the Christian age.

3.) Gentry's third reason for rejecting Double Fulfillment is equally destructive to Dominionism. He says: "The beast belongs to the first century Roman era, irrespective of the many time qualifiers scattered throughout Revelation."

Well, the end of the age belonged to the first century, Old Covenant, Jewish age, "irrespective of the many time qualifiers scattered throughout Revelation"– or the rest of the NT corpus. You cannot divorce the NT discussions of the end of the age from that first century milieu.

So, if one can reject the Double Fulfillment hermeneutic because of the Roman provenance, then upon that identical hermeneutic, one can reject the "AD 70 was a type" claim because it was set specifically in the context of the end of the Old Covenant age of Israel. And remember, McDurmon, (clearly in an unguarded moment) says of the end of the age resurrection prophecy (Matthew 13) that it applied to AD 70 and "should not be understood as teaching anything beyond this."

Gentry has done an excellent job of demonstrating why we have every reason and right to reject the claim that the events of AD 70 were typological of a future eschaton. Furthermore, as we have seen, since the story of Biblical eschatology is a united narrative, one story, then it is patently illogical for the Dominionists to "pick and choose" which elements were typological and which were not.

If the end of the age drama was typological at all, then of necessity: 1.) The New Covenant– which Jesus said would never pass– must nonetheless pass away.

2.) The church will one day become– as the Old Covenant bride became– an unfaithful harlot and Christ will divorce her (and kill her!) and marry another bride, thus establishing another New Covenant.

3.) At the end of the age, the Lord will destroy the current covenant people (due to her covenant unfaithfulness) and create a New People, with a New Name.

These things are not only reprehensible to the gospel message, but, totally unwarranted. There is no justification for the idea the events of AD 70 foreshadowed another end of the age in our future.

How can the Dominionists condemn the dispensational hermeneutic of "Double Fulfillment" whereby they say the first century presence of John as Elijah, and the presence of anti-christs foreshadow a final anti-christ, but then, the Dominionists turn around and tell us the first century, end of the age events were, after all, a foreshadowing of yet future, end of the age events?

To say the least, this is double talk.

## Summary and Conclusion

In this book we have set forth just a few of the many reasons why the proposal of the Amillennial and Postmillennial schools, that AD 70 was typological of a yet future end of the age, end of time event, is false.[205]

It should strike the serious Bible student as strange and significant that there is no attempt on the part of those making the claims to provide any textual, exegetical, substantive proof for their claims. The only two attempts to justify the claim are those made by Jordan whose views we have examined above and shown to be false.

We have shown that Postmillennial writers strongly condemn the dispensational hermeneutic of "Double Fulfillment" of prophecy, calling it unwarranted and unscriptural. And yet, those same writers then turn around and affirm not on the double fulfillment, but, in the words of McDurmon in our debate, multiple fulfillments, fulfillments over and over. To say this is self contradictory, specious and disingenuous is a huge understatement.

We have seen how totally inconsistent and arbitrary the Dominionists are in their application of the multiple fulfillment hermeneutic. On the one hand, they reject the idea that John the Baptizer, as Elijah, the man of sin, the Abomination of Desolation and the Great Tribulation were typological of events to occur at the end of the Christian age.[206]

---

[205] I have catalogued a minimum of at least five more major reasons why AD 70 was not typological, but, I promised myself to keep this book short.

[206] We could have included a discussion of the miraculous outpouring of the Spirit. There is a mixed bag of views in the Postmillennial world about this issue. McDurmon, says it is possible the office of inspired prophet is still operative in the church today, although he (wisely in our view)

They then turn around and claim the end of the age that occurred in AD 70 is typological of the end of the Christian age.

The arbitrary nature of this approach raises serious questions. What is the justification or authority for including some of the "last days" events, but excluding others, which in scripture are every bit as integral to the last days story as the others? You will find no justification for this in any of the Dominionist literature. It is just verbiage and unsubstantiated claims.

Remember, in scripture there is *one end times drama*, one last days, one hope. Yet, the Dominionists especially slice, dice and dichotomize that one story into disparate elements and tenets on what seems like nothing more than the whim of the individual writers. They also have a Genesis eschatology, and a Jewish eschatology, unknown in scripture.[207]

---

refuses to even attempt to find those inspired, authoritative, infallible prophets. On the other hand, Gentry is adamant that the prophetic office has ceased. See his book, *The Charismatic Gift of Prophecy*, available from my websites. What is difficult to find is a Dominionist that takes a firm stand on any future manifestation of the charismata. If the Dominionists reject the first century outpouring of the Spirit as typological, then it becomes just another example of the arbitrary nature of their multiple fulfillment hermeneutic. If they do see the first century events as typological, then it once again raises the issue of how they can reject the man of sin, the Abomination and the Tribulation as typological, and yet include the miraculous outpouring of the Spirit, in a future last days. To say the least, this is just another example of the highly troublesome, self contradictory nature of the multiple fulfillment hermeneutic.

[207] See my arguments in the McDurmon debate. I demonstrated repeatedly that Biblically, there is but one eschatological hope and that was the promises of God made to

As I noted at the beginning, the importance of whether AD 70 was typological can hardly be over-emphasized.

If the Dominionists and Amillennialists can firmly establish that AD 70 and the attendant events were in fact a foreshadowing of yet future events, there is clearly justification for a futurist eschatology– although it would not establish whether it would be Amillennial or Postmillennial.

On the other hand, if it cannot be demonstrated beyond any reasonable doubt that AD 70 was typological then the futurism of these paradigms disappears. There is no future parousia, no future Great White Throne Judgment, no future resurrection, if those things were fulfilled in AD 70. And remember, we have shown that the Dominionists admit these things did in fact have "a fulfillment" at that time. But, there is no "a fulfillment" plus "the fulfillment"of those prophecies.

The NT writers are unambiguous in their declarations that the end of the age was near– and they never speak of another end, of another age. They unequivocally affirm "the" parousia was at hand– and never speak of another parousia. They say, through the revelatory Spirit, the divinely appointed time for the consummation of God's eternal plan was present– and *never* speak of another divinely appointed time. They tell us, using a wide range of time words, terms and phrases, the time for the judgment and resurrection had arrived.[208]

---

Old Covenant Israel in Torah. McDurmon had an Edenic Eschatology, i.e. the solution to the Adamic death, which he posits at the end of human history, and then, he admitted there was an eschatology related to the end of the Old Covenant age in AD 70, i.e. "a fulfillment" of 1 Corinthians 15 / Revelation 20. This is an undeniable rejection of Paul's doctrine of "one hope."

[208] Of course, one of the most popular arguments for a delayed parousia is the issue of the millennium. Per some Amillennialists and Postmillennialists, the millennium *began*

The NT writers never say the eschatological consummation was to be delayed by millennia.[209] In fact, they tell us, "in a very, very little while, the one who is coming will come and will not delay" (Hebrews 10:37).

Our point is the NT writers patently did not look beyond what was happening in their generation to another last days and another eschatological consummation. They said, very clearly, the one eschatological hope foretold– and foreshadowed in the OT– was being fulfilled and was about to be perfected at the imminent parousia.

So, in closing, let me simply list again the reasons why the Amillennial and Postmillennial claims that AD 70 was typological cannot be true:

---

in AD 70, or at least the first century. The millennium must be a long time, we are told, therefore, since the parousia occurs at the end of the millennium, then this proves AD 70 pointed to a different coming, a different judgment, a different resurrection from that which occurred in AD 70. I recommend Joseph Vincent's book, *The Millennium: Past, Present or Future, A Defense of the 40 Year Millennium*, for a refutation of this theory. Also, see my presentation at Criswell College in Dallas, Tx. (2012) on the Preterist Perspective of the Millennium, That presentation definitively demonstrates AD 70 was the end, not the beginning of the millennium. Vincent's book is available from my websites, and when ordered, I will include a free CD of my Criswell presentation.

[209] Gentry and other Dominionists try to find the two millennia delay of the parousia in Matthew 25 claiming the "delay" of the Bridegroom is the so far 2000 year span since Jesus' ascension. This is clearly untenable, since, as we have seen, in scripture, there is but one Wedding, the fulfillment of God's OT promises made to Israel and that was to occur in AD 70. As we have noted above, this is fatal to Gentry's "Wedding" theology.

Reason #1 - The Old Testament prophets never foretold two ends of two ages, two kingdoms, two resurrections or two last days.

Reason #2 - The Christian age has no end. Thus, the end of the Old Covenant age could not be typological of the end of what is endless!

Reason #3 - Types Are Always *Inferior*– Anticipating Something *Better*– and There Is Nothing Better than the Work of Christ in the Church

Reason #4 - No New Testament writer ever said the events of their day were typological of greater events to come.

Reason #5 - Jesus said the events of AD 70 were the greatest that had ever been, or that ever would be (Matthew 24:21). So, how can the greatest events in history, foreshadow events that are even greater?

Reason #6 - Jesus Said the Events of AD 70 Would Be When "All Things That Are Written must Be Fulfilled" (Luke 21:22). This Means There Could Not Be Any Additional Eschatology Beyond Ad 70.

Reason #7– The Restoration of All Things Would Be Consummated at the Parousia– Which Would Be At the End of the Old Covenant Age of Israel

Reason #8 - Paul Said the Goal of All the Previous Ages Had Come in His Generation (1 Corinthians 10:11).

Reason #9 - Then Comes The End – The End of 1 Corinthians 15 Cannot Be the End of Christ's rule or the end of Time.

Reason #10 - Ephesians 1:10 - "That in the stewardship of the fulness of time He would gather together all things in one body, in

Christ."

**Reason #11** - Entrance into the Most Holy Place– Restoraton to the Edenic Presence - The Eschatological Goal Was to Be at the End of the Old Covenant Age– Not the End of the Christian Age (Hebrews 9:6-10).

**Reason #12** - The First Century Church Had Arrived at Zion– The Locus of the Eschatological, End of the Millennium Resurrection.

**Reason #13** - The Judgment of the Living and the Dead Occurred in AD 70 - The Kingdoms of the World Became the Kingdom of God and His Christ.

**Reason #14** - The Millennium Ended in AD 70.

**Reason #15** - If the Events of AD 70 Were Typological of a Future End of the Age, Then Christ Will Divorce and Destroy the Church, as an Unfaithful Bride That Has Become a Harlot and Will Marry Another Bride– Under (Another) New Covenant.

Both individually and collectively these reasons definitively refute and falsify the idea that AD 70 was a type or shadow of the end of the world, the end of human history, the end of the Christian age.

The suggestion and the claim that AD 70 was a typological foreshadowing of the end of time is a theological invention without Biblical merit.

If AD 70 was not a type or foreshadowing of a yet future eschatological consummation, then all futurist paradigms are false.

We have proven there is no Biblical justification for this idea.

AD 70 was the consummation of the "restoration of all things" when man was restored to the Edenic Most Holy Place.

AD 70 was not a type or a foreshadowing of anything!

# Scripture Index

Compiled by Samuel G. Dawson

## Deuteronomy

Dt. 34.1-4  127

## Psalms

Ps. 89.34f  21

## Isaiah

Isaiah 2-4  16, 116, 147
Isa. 2.2  74
Isa. 2.19f  147
Isa. 3.13-24  16
Isaiah 4  158
Isa. 9.6-9  22
Isaiah 24-27  118
Isaiah 25  158
Isaiah 25-27  16
Isa. 25.1-8  56
Isa. 25.6-8  126
Isa. 25.8  52, 119
Isa. 26.19-21  57
Isa. 27.1f  57
Isa. 27.9f  58
Isa. 40.10f  158
Isaiah 62  16
Isa. 62.10f  158
Isa. 65.13  16
Isa. 65.13f  157
Isa. 65.19  11
Isaiah 51  157
Isaiah 52  157
Isaiah 62  157
Isaiah 65-66  71, 157-
    158

## Ezekiel

Ezk. 5.8-9  106, 115
Ezekiel 37  158

## Daniel

Daniel 12  175
Dan. 12.2-7  16, 54

## Hosea

Hos. 10.8  147
Hos. 13.14  52

## Zechariah

Zech. 6.13  158
Zechariah 14  93

## Malachi

Mal. 3.16  63

## Matthew

Mt. 8.29  99
Mt. 11.13-14  154
Mt. 13.11  73
Mt. 16.3  99
Mt. 16.27-28  133, 158
Mt. 17.10f  63
Mt. 17.10-13  154
Mt. 22.1f  16
Mt. 23.29-37  133, 145
Mt. 24.2-3  68
Mt. 24.21  43
Mt. 24.21-27  81
Mt. 24.29-31  47

Mt. 25.1f  85, 170
Mt. 25.31f  23
Mt. 26.18  99

## Luke

Lk. 1.32-35  28
Lk. 12.56  102
Lk. 18.1-8  145
Lk. 19.44  99
Lk. 21.22  49-58
Lk. 23.28-30  147

## Acts

Ac. 3.19-24  59
Ac. 3.23f  15
Ac. 3.24  61
Ac. 13.39  44
Ac. 17.30-31  98, 133
Ac. 24.14-15  15, 51,
    133
Ac. 26.7  70
Ac. 26.21f  15
Ac. 26.21-23  52

## Romans

Rom. 3.26  99
Rom. 5.20-21  44
Rom. 7.4-14  44
Rom. 8.1-3  44
Rom. 8.18  99
Rom. 8.18f  101
Rom. 8.23-9.1-4  52
Rom. 16.20  109

## I Corinthians

I Cor. 1.4-8  80-81
I Cor. 10.6f  36-37
I Cor. 10.11  68-78, 80
I Cor. 13.8f  70, 81
I Cor. 14.36  70
I Cor. 15.23-28  79-95
I Cor. 15.24  22, 24
I Cor. 15.54-55  52
I Cor. 15.55-56  83

## II Corinthians

II Cor. 3.4f  44
II Cor. 4.16f  149
II Cor. 5.17  71

## Galatians

Gal. 3.20-21  44
Gal. 3.23-24  62, 69, 72
Gal. 4.22f  82

## Ephesians

Eph. 1.10  96-104
Eph. 1.3-10  96-104
Eph. 3.20-21  28
Eph. 4.13  70
Eph. 5.25f  85

## Philippians

Phil. 1.6f  104
Phil. 3.11  70

## Colossians

Col. 2.16-17  31

## I Thessalonians

I Thes. 2.16  2
I Thes. 4.13  1
I Thes. 4.13-18  47

## II Thessalonians

II Thes. 1.7f  149

## II Timothy

II Tim. 4.1  133

## Hebrews

Heb. 8.13  159
Heb. 8.13f  40
Heb. 9.8  106
Heb. 9.23f  32
Heb. 10.34f  150
Heb. 11.35  76
Heb. 12.21f  130
Heb. 12.21-23  115

Heb. 12.21-28  28

## James

Jas. 5.6f  150

## I Peter

I Pet. 1.5, 4.1-17  151
I Pet. 1.10-12  61
I Pet. 4.5  61
I Pet. 4.5-17  134
I Pet. 4.7  61, 69
I Pet. 4.17  61, 100

## II Peter

II Pet. 3.1-2, 13  15

## Revelation

Rev. 1.3  100
Rev. 6.10-11  148
Rev. 6.12f  148
Rev. 10.7  15
Rev. 11.15  111
Rev. 11.15f  136
Rev. 11.15-18  25
Rev. 15.8  111
Rev. 19.6f  85
Rev. 22.1-3  26
Rev. 22.3-4  22
Revelation 20  16

# Topic Index

Compiled by Samuel G. Dawson

*1-2 Thessalonians, The IVP New Testament Series*, Greg Beale 47

## A

*A Case for Amillennialism*, Kim Riddlebarger 5
abomination of desolation, element of eschatology 155
Abraham
at kingdom table 126
received land through his descendants 127
AD70
amillennialists on 17
and the end of the millennium 141-152
and the marriage of Christ and the church 153-179
Beale thinks type of the end of the world 5
Boettner denies double fulfillment paradigm 9
Christ married church in 171
covenantal significance of 44
DeMar and McDurmon say entirety AD70 170
dispensationalists don't often speak of it's being type of the real end 6
dominionists view of typological 162-165
early church had no double fulfillment paradigm 10
evangelical realization of eschatological significance of 1

events of were greatest, not typical 43-48
first century church had arrived at Zion 115-131
fulness of time not initiated by, but accomplished 98
Gentry, Kenneth
applies Dan 12.2 to 54
thinks type of final judgment 4
goal of all previous ages 68-78
Hanegraaff thinks type of the end of the world 5
Ice thinks total fulfillment of prophecies of Israel 6
if typological, church will be destroyed 177
Jesus applied Isaiah 2 to 117
judgment occurred at 132-140
McDurmon, Joel
attacks double fulfillment eschatology 8
believes multiple fulfillments 9
no fulfillments beyond 49-58
no New Testament writer said events of their day were typological 36-42
North thinks type of final tribulation 4
not type of anything 16
*parousia* consummated at 59-67
postmillennialists affirm typical of future events 7
prophets never foretold ends of two ages 15-20
resurrection posited at 56

then comes the end  79-95
type of the real end of the age?  3
types are always inferior  30-35
wouldn't end of time be greater
than fall of Jerusalem  45
Adamic death
amillennialists on  17
discussed  84, 106
futurists believe was physical
death  13
resurrection from  84
adoption was the resurrection  52
age to come
goal of all previous ages  71
McDurmon on  72
two?  75
all in all, God, fulfillment of
Zechariah 14  93
amillennialists
on Adamic Curse and AD70  17
use gaps themselves  117
view of Isaiah 2-4  117
*Analytical Lexicon of New Testa-
ment Greek*, Robinson and House,
on *mello*  133
*Apocalypse Code*, Hank Hanegraaff
5
*Arndt and Gingrich Greek Lexicon*
70
ascension, Gentry says *parousia* not
imminent since  170
Athanasius rejected double fulfillment paradigm  10
Aune, David  *Word Biblical Commentary, Revelation, Vol. 52c*  142

**B**

Babylon
dominionists say is Old Covenant
Jerusalem  93
Mathison's vacillation on identity
of  111
Bahnsen, Greg  *From Age to Age:
The Unfolding of Biblical Escha-
tology*  31

Bahnsen, Greg  *Theonomy in Chris-
tian Ethics*  32
Bahnsen, Greg, sabbath of Torah vs.
Christian sabbath  11
Barton, John  *The Biblical World*  37
Barton, John, on I Cor. 10.6f  37
*Bauer, Arndt and Gingrich Greek
Lexicon*  70
Beale, Greg
on Garden as most holy place
105
parallels Matthew 24 and I and II
Thessalonians  47
thinks AD70 is type of the end of
the world  5
Beale, Greg  *1-2 Thessalonians, The
IVP New Testament Series*  47
Beale, Greg  *New International
Greek Testament Commentary*  26,
142
Beale, Greg  *The Temple and the
Church's Mission*  5, 105
*Before Jerusalem Fell*, Kenneth Gen-
try  111
better resurrection
discussed  76
if fulfilled, what better resurrection awaits?  167
Blaising, Craig  *Three Views of the
Millennium and Beyond*  142
Boettner, Lorraine  *The Meaning of
the Millennium, Four Views*  9
Boettner, Lorraine, denies double
fulfillment paradigm  9
Bruce, F. F.  *The Time is Fulfilled*
100
Christian age
has no end  21-29
Mosaic age the only interim age
98
not an interim age  98
church
AD70 and the marriage of Christ
and the  153-179
Christ married in AD70  171

destroyed if AD70 typological
177
Pentecost says a mystery 73
church age, premillennialists say not
the kingdom age 74
church, the, anticipated destiny of
previous ages 76

# C

Cochrane, Arthur C. *Reformed Confessions of the 16th Century* 41-42
*Commentary on the New Testament
Use of the Old Testament*, Jeffrey
Wiema 47
*Conversion of the Imagination*, Richard Hays 36
corporate body
Gentry on resurrection of 156
resurrection of 156
covenant eschatology vs preterism 3
creeds
appeal of dominionists and premillennialists to 41-42
premillennialism condemned in
some 41-42
Daniel 7, source for Revelation 20
142

# D

Davies, W. D. and Dale Allison *International Critical Commentary,
Matthew 1-7* 64
day of the Lord, N. T. Wright on 1
delivering the kingdom
is not abdication 91
Wayne Jackson says the end of
Christ's rule 91
DeMar, Gary
entirety of Olivet Discourse
speaks of AD70 170
McDurmon's employer rejects
his hermeneutic 122
on age to come 41
on abomination of desolation 155
on end of the age 159

on *kairos* 101
on man of sin 156
on Romans 8 101
parallels Matthew 24 and I and II
Thessalonians 46
says all promises to Old Covenant Israel fulfilled 124
DeMar, Gary *Last Days Madness*
44, 47, 159
*Dispensationalism, Rightly Dividing
the People of God?*, Keith
Mathison 5, 160
dispensationalists
don't often speak of AD70 being
typological of the real end 6
Gentry rejects double-fulfillment
paradigm 172
*Dominion and Common Grace*,
Gary North 4
*Dominion*, Kenneth Gentry 157
dominionists
*See also* postmillennialists
appeal to creeds 41-42
arbitrary and capricious in application of typology 162
changing on Daniel 12 175
condemn double fulfillment paradigm 10
contradict themselves on double
fulfillment eschatology 12
differ strongly on the harvest 88
general agreements with important elements of eschatology
153
insist on multiple fulfillment of
prophecy 65
mass confusion about the Law of
Moses 84
mixed bag on miraculous outpouring of Holy Spirit 180
most agree on man of sin 156
pick and choose which elements
of eschatology typological 162-
165
pick and choose which elements
of eschatology typological 178

restoration of all things began in
  first century  60
say Babylon is Old Covenant Jerusalem  93
say Ephesians 1 is the final eschatological event  97
trapped by inconsistencies on
  time stements  173
two great commissions?  161
vacillation on mello  133
view of Zion  123
double fulfillment eschatology
  Athanasius rejected  10
  dominionists contradict them-
    selves on  12
  early church had none  10
  Gentry, Kenneth
    attacks  8
    rejects dispensational para-
      digm  172
    hermeneutic of  178
  McDurmon, Joel
    attacks  8
    believes multiple fulfillments
      9
  prophets never foretold ends of
    two ages  15-20
  Theoderet of Cyprus rejected  10

## E

Elijah
  element of eschatology  154
  Gentry on appearance of  154
  Mathison on appearance of  154
Ellingworth, Charles *New International Greek Testament Commentary*  107
end
  Christian age has no  21-29
  fulfillment of hope of Israel  81
  futurist views say no evangelism
    after the  28
  life continues after the of Revela-
    tion 20  22
  of Revelation 20  22

of the Christian age?  68
of time?  81
then comes the  79-95
typological?  80
end of the age
  DeMar agrees with Gentry  159
  element of eschatology  159
end of time, futurist eschatologies
  and the  59
end, the
  end of Torah  83
  Gentry says wedding of Matthew
    25 is the true one  86
  is not the end of Christ's rule  91
  the harvest  88
  the wedding  85
Engelsma, David, denies unity of
  Matthew 24  46
Ephesians 1, dominionists say it's
  the final eschatological event  97
eschatology
  elements of
    abomination of desolation  155
    appearance of Elijah  154
    church fathers believed all
      these tents fulfilled in first
      century  160
    discussed  154-165
    dominionists pick and choose
      which typological  162-165
    end of the age  159
    great commission  160
    great tribulation  156
    judgment coming of the Lord
      158
    man of sin  156
    Messianic banquet  158
    Messianic marriage  157
    Messianic temple  158
    new creation  157
    New Jerusalem  157
    passing of heaven and earth
      157
    resurrection of the dead  156
    wedding not minor  172

Jewish thought is one organic
drama 175
no new in New Testament 53
eschatons, prophets didn't foretell
two 15
eternal purpose of God
discussed 96-104
goal of all previous ages 73
not indicative of a greater eternal
purpose 97
evangelism, futurists say none after
the end 28
*Expositors Greek Testament*, Robertson Nicoll 107

## F

final, McDurmon's inconsistent use
of 121
*Four Views of Revelation*, Kenneth
Gentry 10
*From Age to Age: The Unfolding of
Biblical Eschatology*, Greg
Bahnsen 31
Frost, Sam, on Revelation 11 137
fulness of time
Christ appeared in the 103
last days of Mosaic age 103
not initiated by AD70, but perfected 98
stewardship of 96-104
futurist views
believe death of Adam was physical death 13
greater than those of Mt. 24.21
44
say no evangelism after the end
28

## G

Garden of Eden is the most holy
place 104
Gentry, Kenneth
adamant prophetic office has
ceased 181
applies Dan. 12.2

to AD70 54
to end of world 54
to resurrection of Israel 54
attacks dispensational paradigm 7
Christ's return not imminent
since ascension 170
destroys his own postmillennial
futurist eschatology 58
doesn't mention Isaiah 25-27 58
double-minded on world mission
161
no eschaton beyond Israel's last
days 17
on appearance of Elijah 154
on end of the age 159
on end of the age in Matthew 13
88
on eschatological signifiance of
AD70 1
on great tribulation 156
on Lk. 21.22 49
on new creation 157
on resurrection of corporate body
156
on Rom. 16.20 110
on significance of kairos 100
on world mission 160
parallels Matthew 24 and I and II
Thessalonians 47
rejects dispensational double fulfillment paradigm 172
significance of John the Baptist
64
two weddings, two brides, two
comings? 86
vacillation on mello 134
wedding of Matthew 25 is the
true end 86
Gentry, Kenneth *Before Jerusalem
Fell* 111
Gentry, Kenneth *Dominion* 157
Gentry, Kenneth *Four Views of
Revelation* 10
Gentry, Kenneth *He Shall Have Dominion* 1, 44

Gentry, Kenneth  *Perilous Times, A Study in Eschatological Evil*  7, 173
Gentry, Kenneth  *Revelation Made Easy*  4
Gentry, Kenneth  *The Great Tribulation: Past or Future, Two Evangelicals Debate the Question*  1
Gentry, Kenneth  *Thine Is the Kingdom*  4, 47
Gentry, Kenneth and Thomas Ice  *The Great Tribulation, Past or Future?*  6, 159
Gibbs, Jeffrey A.  *Jerusalem and Parousia*  92
goal of all previous ages
  discussed  68-78
  God's eternal purpose  73
  kingdom of God  73
  new covenant world  72
  new creation  71
  only forty years?  75
  resurrection  71
  the age to come  71
  the church  76
  was being achieved  71
  what was it?  71
God all in all, fulfillment of Zechariah 14  93
God's eternal purpose, goal of all previous ages  73
Goppelt, Leonhard  *Typos The Typological Interpretation of the Old Testament in the New*  36
great commission
  element of eschatology  160
  two?  161
Great Day of the Lord, Rev. 6.12f  148
great tribulation
  element of eschatology  156
  Gentry on  156
  Mathison on  156
  North on  156
  tied to resurrection at end of millennium  176

*Great Tribulation: Past or Future, Two Evangelicals Debate the Question*, Kenneth Gentry  1

**H**

Hagner, Donald  *Word Biblical Commentary, Matthew, Vol. 33*  63
Hanegraaff, Hank  *Apocalypse Code*  5
Hanegraaff, Hank, thinks AD70 is type of the end of the world  5
harvest
  dominionists differ strongly on  88
  Leithbart on  88
  Revelation 14 on  88
  the end is the  88
Hays, Richard  *Conversion of the Imagination*  36
*He Shall Have Dominion*, Kenneth Gentry  1, 44
heaven and earth, passing of
  element of eschatology  157
  Seriah on  169
hope of Israel, the end the fulfillment of the  81
*Hope*, Keith Mathison  86
hopes, two?  75

**I**

I Corinthians 15, Zechariah 14 a thumbnail sketch of  94
Ice, Thomas and Kenneth Gentry  *The Great Tribulation, Past or Future?*  6
Ice, Thomas, thinks total fulfillment of prophecies of Israel in AD70  6
*International Critical Commentary, Matthew 1-7*, W. D. Davies and Dale Allison  64
Israel
  about to be cast out  83
  McDurmon says God's people until resurrection  82

# J

Jackson, Wayne
   Christ not ruling after his coming 22
   the end is the end of Christ's rule 91
Jackson, Wayne *The AD 70 Theory: A Review of The Max King Doctrine* 23, 91
*Jerusalem and Parousia*, Jeffrey A. Gibbs 92
Jerusalem, Riddlebarger thinks a type of last days apostate church 5
*Jesus and the Victory of God*, N. T. Wright 2
*Jesus v. Jerusalem*, Joel McDurmon 8, 155
Jews, hold eschatology as one organic drama 175
John the Baptist
   as Elijah a sign of two Great Days of the Lord? 65
   eschatological significance of 62
   Gentry on significance of 64
Jordan, James, on types always pointing to something better 33
judgment coming of the Lord
   element of eschatology 158
judgment, the
   final, Gentry thinks AD70 a type of 4
   in context of Isaiah 2-4 116
   Nicene Creed on 132
   occurred in AD70 132-140
   of I Pet. 4.5-17 134

# K

*kairos*
   DeMar on 101
   discussion of importance of 98
   Gentry on significance of 100
kingdom
   delivery is not abdication 91
   goal of all previous ages 73
   Zion the locus of 118
   kingdom age, premillennialists say not the church age 74

# L

Lane, William *Word Biblical Commentary, Hebrews 9-13* 107
*Last Days Madness*, Gary DeMar 44, 47, 159
Law of Moses, dominionists' mass confusion about 84
Leitbart, Peter *The Promise of His Coming* 88
Leitbart, Peter, on the harvest 88
*Like Father Like Son, On Clouds of Glory*, Don K. Preston 3

# M

man of sin
   DeMar on 156
   element of eschatology 156
   Gentry on 156
martyr vindication
   at end of millennium 151
   Daniel 7 source of Revelation 20 142
   imminent in first century 149
   Isaiah 2-4 and 147
   key to understanding the millennium 141
   Lk. 18.1-8 and 145
   none separate from Moses, Isaiah, Paul, James, or Peter 151
   theme of 143
   united testimony of Moses, Isaiah, Jesus, Paul, James, and Peter 151
Mathison, Keith
   on abomination of desolation 155
   on appearance of Elijah 154
   on great tribulation 156
   on the judgment and the Nicene Creed 132

vacillation on identify of Babylon
111
Mathison, Keith *Dispensationalism,
Rightly Dividing the People of
God?* 160
Mathison, Keith *Postmillennialism:
An Eschatology of Hope* 45, 124,
132
Mathison, Keith, *Dispensationalism:
Rightly Dividing the House of God*
5
Mathison, Keith, *Hope* 86
Mbuvi, Andrew M. *Temple, Exile,
and Identify in I Peter* 37
McDurmon, Joel
  argues for fulfillment of Zion
    promises 125
  attacks double fulfillment double-
    cross 8
  attacks double fulfillment escha-
    tology 8
  employer DeMar rejects his her-
    meneutic 122
  entirety of Olivet Discourse
    speaks of AD70 170
  inconsistent use of final 121
  Israel God's people until resurrec-
    tion 82
  multiple fulfillments of I Corin-
    thians 15 and Revelation 20 39
  on abomination of desolation 155
  on age to come 72
  on Heb. 8.13 159
  on Heb. 8.13f 40
  on *kairos* 102
  on Lk. 12.56 102
  on multiple fulfillments of proph-
    ecy 155
  on prophetic office still operating
    181
  on resurrection 157
  on wedding parable of Matthew
    22 166
  on world mission 160
McDurmon, Joel *Jesus v. Jerusalem*
8, 155

*mello*
  Blass-DeBrunner Grammar on
    133
  Robinson and House, *Analytical
    Lexicon of New Testament
    Greek* on 133
  vacillation of dominionists on
    133
  vacillation of Gentry on 134
Messianic banquet, element of eschatology 158
Messianic marriage, element of eschatology 158
Messianic temple, element of eschatology 158
millennium
  AD70 and the end of the 141-152
  Gentry on 142
  Joseph Vincent on 141
  martyr vindication at end of the
    151
  martyr vindication key to under-
    standing the 141
  tribulation tied to resurrection at
    end of 176
Mosaic age
  fullness of time the last days of
    103
  most holy place entered at end of
    105-114
  only interim age 98
most holy place
  Beale on Garden as the 105
  entered at the end of the Mosaic
    Age 105-114
  Garden of Eden was 104

**N**

new covenant world, goal of all previous ages 72
new creation
  element of eschatology 157
  Gentry on 157
  goal of all previous ages 71
new heaven and earth

prophets foretold 16
when God establishes 34
*New International Greek Testament Commentary*, Charles Ellingworth 107
*New International Greek Testament Commentary*, Greg Beale 26, 142
New Jerusalem, element of eschatology 158
New Testament
no new eschatology in 53
no writer said events of their day were typological 36-42
Nicene Creed
on the judgment 132
premillennialism condemned in 41-42
Nicoll, Robertson *Expositors Greek Testament* 107
North, Gary *Dominion and Common Grace* 4

### O

Old Covenant, the end of the 83
Olivet Discourse, DeMar and McDurmon say entirety is AD70 170
one hope, not two in two eschatons 18-19

### P

*parousia*
consummated at AD70 59-67
Gentry says not imminent since ascension 170
is the time of the wedding 23
*Paul*, N. T. Wright 2
Pentecost, Dwight *Things to Come* 73
Pentecost, Dwight, the church age a mystery 73
*Perilous Times, A Study in Eschatological Evil*, Kenneth Gentry 7, 173
postmillennialism

changing on Daniel 12 175
mixed bag on miraculous outpouring of Holy Spirit 180
*Postmillennialism: An Eschatology of Hope*, Keith Mathison 45, 124, 132
postmillennialists
affirm AD70 was typical of future events 7
growing number accept unity of Matthew 24 45
premillennialism
condemned in some creeds 41-42
appeal to creeds 41-42
church age not the kingdom age 74
Preston, Don K. *Like Father Like Son, On Clouds of Glory* 3
Preston, Don K. *We Shall Meet Him In The Air, The Wedding of the King of Kings* 13
preterism vs. covenant eschatology 3
prophetic office
Gentry adamant it has ceased 181
McDurmon on present operation 181

### R

*Reformed Confessions of the 16th Century*, Arthur C. Cochrane 41-42
restoration of all things, dominionists see beginning in first century 60
resurrection
element of eschatology 156
from Adamic death 84
Gentry on corporate body 156
goal of all previous ages 72
I Corinthians 15 the final 85
if better one fulfilled, what better resurrection awaits 167
McDurmon on 157

McDurmon says Israel God's people until 82
prophets foretold 16
repeatedly posited at AD70 56
Revelation 20 16
tied to great tribulation at end of millennium 176
return of Christ, Gentry says not imminent since ascension 170
Revelation 20, Daniel 7 source of 142
Revelation 20-22, Zechariah 14 a thumbnail sketch of 94
*Revelation Made Easy*, Kenneth Gentry 4
Riddlebarger, Kim
   double fulfillment of Mt. 24.21 44
   thinks Jerusalem and temple a type of last days apostate church 5
Riddlebarger, Kim *A Case for Amillennialism* 5
Robertson, John A. T. *Word Pictures in the New Testament* 107
Robinson and House, *Analytical Lexicon of New Testament Greek*, on *mello* 133

**S**

sabbath
   Bahnsen on 31
   Bahnsen on Torah sabbath vs. Christian 11
   typological important in eschatology 112
Seriah, Jonathin, on passing of heaven and earth 169
Sproul, R. C. *The Last Days According to Jesus* 1
Sproul, R. C., on eschatological significance of AD70 1
temple
   Riddlebarger thinks a type of last days apostate church 5

theological center of the earth 115

**T**

*Temple, Exile, and Identity in I Peter* 38
*The AD 70 Theory: A Review of The Max King Doctrine*, Wayne Jackson 23, 91
*The Biblical World*, John Barton 37
*The Great Tribulation, Past or Future?* Kenneth Gentry and Thomas Ice 159
*The Land Called Holy, Palestine in Christian History and Thought*, Robert Wilken 10, 37
*The Last Days According to Jesus*, R. C. Sproul 1
*The Meaning of the Millennium, Four Views*, Lorraine Boettner 9
*The Millennium: Past, Present or Future?* Joseph Vincent 141
*The Temple and the Church's Mission*, Greg Beale 5, 105
*The Time is Fulfilled*, F. F. Bruce 100
Theoderet of Cyprus, rejected double fulfillment paradigm 10
*Theonomy in Christian Ethics*, Greg Bahnsen 32
*Thine Is the Kingdom*, Kenneth Gentry 4, 47
*Things to Come*, Dwight Pentecost 73
*Three Views of the Millennium and Beyond*, Craig Blaising 142
Torah, the end of 83
tribulation, North thinks AD70 type of final 4
types
   always inferior 30-35
   early church believed they were not 37
   II Peter 3 and 38

James Jorden believes always point to something better 33
John Barton on 37
Mbuvi on 37
Robert Wilken on 37
those in Old Covenant pointed to something better 33
typological sabbath, important in eschatology 112
*Typos The Typological Interpretatino of the Old Testament in the New*, Leonhard Goppelt 36

**V**

Vincent, Joseph *The Millennium: Past, Present or Future?* 141
Vincent, Joseph, on the millennium 141

**W**

*We Shall Meet Him In The Air, The Wedding of the King of* Kings, Don K. Preston 13
wedding of Messiah
AD70 and the marriage of Christ and the church 153-179
Christ married church in AD70 171
discussed 16
Gentry says wedding of Matthew 25 is the true end 86
not minor, but foundational element of eschatology 171
parousia is time of 24
the end is 85
Weima, Jeffrey, parallels Matthew 24 and I and II Thessalonians 47
Wiema, Jefffrey *Commentary on the New Testament Use of the Old Testament* 47
Wilken, Robert *The Land Called Holy, Palestine in Christian History and Thought* 10, 37
Wilken, Robert, on Old Testament types in the New Testament 37

*Word Biblical Commentary, Hebrews 9-13*, William Lane 107
*Word Biblical Commentary, Matthew, Vol. 33*, Donald Hagner 63
*Word Pictures in the New Testament*, John A. T., Robertson 107
*World Biblical Commentary, Revelation, Vol. 52c*, David Aune 142
world mission
Gentry double-minded on 161
Gentry on 160
implications of saying AD70 typological 161
Wright, N. T.
on eschatological signifiance of AD70 1
on I Thes. 2.16 2
on I Thes. 4.13 1
Wright, N. T. *Jesus and the Victory of God* 2
Wright, N. T. *Paul* 2

**Z**

Zechariah 14
a thumbnail sketch
of I Corinthians 15 94
of Revelation 20-22 94
dominionist view of 123
first century church had arrived at Zion 115-131
Hebrews author on 128
Isaiah 24-27 contains an important prophecy of 118
locus of the kingdom 118
McDurmon argues for fulfillment of promises of 125
significance of 115

Made in the USA
Lexington, KY
19 June 2013